MW00623081

# THE SECOND AMENDMENT

## UNDER ATTACK FROM ALL ANGLES

by Arthur R. Thompson

Published by
The John Birch Society
Appleton, Wisconsin

First Printing . . . . . . . . . . . . . . . . . . . . . . . . . May, 2020
Second Printing . . . . . . . . . . . . . . . . . . . . . . . July, 2021

Published by
The John Birch Society
770 N. Westhill Boulevard
Appleton, Wisconsin 54914
www.JBS.org

Library of Congress Control Number: 2021937826
International Standard Book Number (ISBN): 978-1-881919-14-8

Printed in the United States of America

Cover Design: Nilai Lee
Photo Credits: DNY59/ iStock / Getty Images Plus,
blackred / iStock / Getty Images Plus

# CONTENTS

# INTRODUCTION

The American system of government is different from any other on the planet.

Some believe that the main difference is the fact that we are an armed people — or at least have the ability and right to be armed — that we have a Bill of Rights that protects our right to keep and bear arms, and that this is the paramount right.

This idea is only partially true.

Before the firm advocate of the Second Amendment throws this book down, allow us to explain.

Note that the Bill of Rights has a number of rights that are enumerated before the right to keep and bear arms. These are the right to practice one's religion and to assemble to do so, to freedom of speech and the press, to peacefully assemble, and to petition the government for a redress of grievances.

These are indeed important rights; however, the rights that come after them are important as well, and are based on a number of principles on which our government was founded.

We will expound on these rights as well as we go through our dissertation, because they are all interlocked. No single right is paramount over another. They are all equal, since no right can cancel out another right or we have no rights at all. The erosion of one right will lead to the erosion of the others. We will demonstrate as we go along how this can happen.

There are aspects of our rights that affect our right to keep and bear arms that are not generally known by most Americans. We shall expound on these aspects to show how they are interrelated to the Second Amendment and that the Second cannot stand by itself.

*Where do we get our rights?*

What is a right anyway?

We start with the Declaration of Independence, which gives us the answers to these questions.

The Declaration was the document that justified waging the War for Independence, and formed our country, before we had either the Articles of Confederation or the Constitution.

Let us start with the second paragraph of the Declaration of Independence, because it explains the source of our rights.

It states:

> We hold these truths to be self-evident, that all Men are created equal, that they are endowed by their Creator with certain unalienable Rights, that among these are Life, Liberty, and the Pursuit of Happiness.

This statement means that we get our rights from God. If they come from God, then no man or government may rightly deprive men of them. This was a major foundation for our revolution against our government at the time, that of Great Britain.

The Declaration declares we have rights and they do not come from government or a king.

The Declaration served and serves as the basic rock on which our government rests, followed by the Constitution. Yet, as we shall see, this rock is becoming cracked as it is pounded away at by those who want to deprive us of our rights and change American society into a Marxist state on the road to their New World Order.

Far too many people today have not received a good understanding of these two primary documents — the Declaration and Constitution — in their education. This has been a problem for some time, probably more years than the average person realizes. The proof of this is seen in the steady erosion of the rights delineated in the Constitution and the usurpation of powers by government that are not delegated to the government in the Constitution.

In other words, the government has been taking upon itself powers that are not allowed in the Constitution. With each assumption of power, it simultaneously diminishes the rights of the people.

One would think that if the majority of the people *understood* the Constitution, they would make Congress and the government officials adhere to it.

We used the word *understood*. Understanding is more than simply reading. Understanding is grasping and comprehending the wisdom of how and why the Constitution was written as it was.

Only by understanding these things can one appreciate the full meaning of the Second Amendment.

There are constant attacks on our rights in today's political atmosphere. These attacks are not only on our Second Amendment rights, but on all of our rights, some of which have been eroded to the point of being nearly nonexistent, such as property rights. Once a right is eliminated, the absence of that right can be used to negate others, including the Second Amendment.

So an understanding of all of our rights must be included in the study of the Second Amendment.

First of all, let us use examples of where an authoritarian government could confiscate the arms of the people in short order. Do not scoff at these examples; we will show that they are real possibilities.

What would you do if the authorities called up and said that they have your children at school and they will not be allowed to return home until you come and turn in your arms?

What if the authorities shut off your electricity in the dead of winter and told you that you would not have power restored until you turned in your arms?

What if the authorities required your neighbors to turn in their arms, and when they did (or even if they did not have any), then asked them to name which of their neighbors possess firearms?

What if the authorities took away the ownership rights to your property, and would not restore them to you until your turned in your arms?

What if the authorities surrounded a two-by-two-block area, moved all of the people out, and put them in a holding area until they searched every residence looking for evidence of anti-government literature or items that had been banned from private ownership?

The latter happened to an acquaintance of this author in Austria after the *Anschluss* takeover by the German National Socialists. It happened so rapidly there was no way of escape or of being able to hide anything that was deemed unlawful. His brother had connections to someone in Nazi leadership, so he packed his bags and left the country while the borders were still open enough to do so. He never returned, and ultimately ended up in the United States.

All totalitarian states use the schools to turn children against their parents. This technique was famous in Nazi Germany, and in the Soviet Union statues were erected of a communist Young Pioneer member who ratted out his parents, as an example for other youth to follow. What if your own child told the authorities that you had an "illegal" weapon?

There are all sorts of ways to get people to meekly give up their weapons, especially if they are isolated from like-minded Americans in their desire to resist unconstitutional actions by the government.

What if your neighborhood was in flames due to rioters? You would protect your home. But, what if the authorities came through and in the name of quelling the violence, even took the weapons of the homeowners who had nothing to do with the violence?

This is not all that unrealistic when you consider that a couple in St. Louis in 2020, who defended their home by brandishing some firearms, had their weapons confiscated and were charged with a crime when they did nothing but defend their home from a violent mob.

They stood alone. Even their neighbors were mad at them because they believed the homeowners were to blame for a possible escalation of the situation — even when that escalation didn't happen — because the couple were armed. The neighbors were so afraid of the mob that they turned on their neighbors for fear that the mob might turn on them.

It is an example of a single person or family facing powerful influences against acting on their own. If their neighbors turn on them out of fear of the mob or the authorities, then they would be truly alone. Then what? Will they — you — act alone with no support around you? Will you stand up for your rights when the whole world seems against you? When you possibly could be killed, leaving your family with no one to help them?

These are examples of how other rights that have been abrogated can be used to disarm the people.

The bumper sticker that says that they won't get your gun until they pry it from your cold, dead hands is very macho, but unrealistic. They have ways to get you to meekly turn in your gun and be thankful they don't punish you for doing so in the process.

If you are alone.

By now, your blood pressure is probably above normal. You are muttering to yourself that they will never be able to do that to you.

Are you really different from millions of other people who have turned in their weapons around the world? People who thought they lived in free countries, but when the laws were passed to disarm the citizenry, went to their closets, picked up their guns, and turned them in at the local police station? This has happened in such countries as Britain, Australia, and others, countries that had all of the trappings of liberty, except they weren't really free. It only looked as if they were.

They were relatively free at one time, but what happened?

What happened was that the people lost their freedom because they lost their understanding of what freedom is and how to keep it.

Once the people were "educated" away from understanding what freedom is and how to preserve it, they became isolated in their communities, not organized in any fashion to work together to gain back their freedom.

Does this sound familiar?

It is what is happening in America.

It is because the people are no longer taught an *understanding* of the basic documents of the United States: the Declaration of Independence, the Constitution, and the Bill of Rights.

In addition, the people have become divided, no longer acting as neighbors, sometimes not even knowing the name of their next-door neighbor.

How can you get your neighbors to stand up for each other if they do not even know one another?

Rioters in the cities can get away with doing what they do because most people cower in their homes, afraid to "make any waves" in the hope that the mob will pass them by.

The neighbors do not even know each other's telephone numbers to call and work together in a crisis — any crisis.

That bumper sticker doesn't work — well, maybe it does, but you would be alone and they *would* pry your gun out of your cold, dead hands.

While these things may seem a bit extreme, we are witnessing extremism in our communities, with a growing demand that we either downsize local police or get rid of them entirely.

If we cannot rely on our police, our neighbors, or ourselves to defend us from the criminal or rioter, we are in serious trouble.

Something is vitally wrong and needs to be fixed.

We will explore what is wrong and how to fix it, primarily as is reflected in preserving the Second Amendment.

# Chapter One

# WHENCE COMES THE ATTACK ON OUR RIGHTS

Most Americans are not aware that there is a *systematic attack* on our rights. The diminishing of our rights has not been done by accident or by the natural evolution of civilization or history.

The basic reason for this includes the fact that many no longer have a full understanding of what their rights are. They have never been taught in school nor have they adequately studied the basic documents of our country and what they all mean — the principles on which they stand.

Nor have they realized that there are organized groups of people who want to end what we call America and American exceptionalism — although some began to see this as hundreds of mobs in the streets in 2020 obviously wanted to tear down everything.

At first these mobs were called anarchists, but as time went by it became obvious that they were led not by anarchists but by Marxists. So where did these Marxists come from all of a sudden? How did they get so organized as to spring up in city after city *all demanding the same things at the same time?*

They have been here all of the time, educating and organizing our youth in the schools, etc. What we saw is the fruit of that education.

One of the main tactics used by the communists has been to infiltrate the schools and produce young communists. In foreign countries it has not been unusual for students imbued with communism to flow out of the schools and provide the street mobs for revolution. The same tactic has been in use in this country for decades, though we are only now seeing the results of that labor.

This author used to speak in schools in his large city and witnessed certain teachers who spent their time teaching anti-Americanism and communism to the students. They often had to give a "balance" to their treason by inviting in someone to represent the other side, and we provided that balance, sometimes under very uncomfortable circumstances.

During the War in Vietnam you could see classrooms decked out as if they were the Vietcong, with pictures of Ho Chi Minh and Mao Zedong, and study halls with tables of the communist-led Students for a Democratic Society, with communist literature available for the students. In one case, the high-school study hall was on the ground floor. Parents saw the room and started to complain, so the school authorities moved the study hall up a couple of floors to keep the parents unaware of what was going on in their local school.

This sort of thing was not unusual. It happened in the City of Seattle, and was embedded in several high schools. Is it any wonder Seattle had the problems it had in 2020, with the declaration of a section of the city as a free country called the Capitol Hill Autonomous Zone, then renamed the Capitol Hill Occupied Protest, or CHOP?

The reference to CHOP harkened back to the French Revolution, when the guillotine was in use. There was even video from Seattle that showed one of the revolutionaries singing about what the French did in the revolution: chop.

This was not unusual. In the demonstrations a few weeks later in Portland, Oregon, a guillotine was rolled out into the street before the police bureau and American flags were burned at its base. It was a message as to what they wanted to do to the police and anyone else who opposed them.

Portland was not the only place where references to the guillotine were used.

Every radical organization of any size claims to harken back to the French Revolution.

This is interesting because Americans had a problem with the French Revolutionaries at the very beginning of our country. This is a part of our history that has become hidden from the American people over time.

There has been a systematic campaign by the socialists to alter and distort American history. While they have elevated socialists as heroes, they have at the same time eliminated the real heroes from the history books, or maligned them in the eyes of the students. Thus we witnessed the tearing down of statues around the country in 2020.

While statues of American heroes were being pulled down or desecrated, in Seattle the statue of the Russian communist revolutionary leader Lenin remained erect and even had flowers placed at its base.

In the mid-1800s, the influence of Karl Marx started to grow in the United States. As it grew, there began a campaign against the rights delineated in the Bill of Rights. It was subtle, but effective over a period of time.

For those who doubt that the Marxists had influence in our country that far back, it must be noted that Marx wrote for eleven years before the Civil War for the *New-York Tribune*, the paper with the largest circulation in the country for a Sunday edition. The publisher of the newspaper, Horace Greeley, joined the Communist International and later ran against Ulysses S. Grant for president on the Democratic ticket.

You probably didn't hear about this in your history class in school.*

We do not want to get too far afield in our explanation about the whys and wherefores of how our rights have come under attack, but there was a campaign by Marxists to so alter the American system that there would be no stopping the communist takeover of America — doing it so slowly and subtly that the people would not notice it until it was too late.

Americans need to understand our history so they will be forearmed to be able to protect our rights.

Knowing historical facts is not enough; one must *under-*

---

* For a comprehensive look at the early history of America from the standpoint of the attacks against God and the Constitution during the first one hundred years of our history, read *To the Victor Go the Myths & Monuments*, available from ShopJBS.org.

*stand* history in order to preserve freedom.

George Orwell, the author of the important novels *1984* and *Animal Farm*, said it well:

> The most effective way to destroy people is to deny and obliterate their own understanding of their history.

Orwell was a man who cooperated with the communists before World War II, and he understood the direction they were going, and what they were doing to get there. He broke with them and penned the books that made him famous. These books warned the people of what the Marxists' plans were and how their plans would lead the people into bondage.

The idea of understanding history has long been crucial to people preserving their liberty and heritage. Two thousand years ago Cicero, the great Roman orator and senator, tried to save the Roman republic from deteriorating into a democracy on the road to an imperial government under the emperors. He was murdered in the attempt.

Cicero said:

> To be ignorant of what occurred before you were born is to remain always a child.

Even two thousand years ago, the lack of education was noted as a problem in preserving a sound government.

Many of you will not believe the history that we point out because it is too alien to what you have been taught.

Mark Twain had something to say about that:

> The only difference between reality and fiction is that fiction needs to be credible.

People are being programmed to reject conspiracies, simply because conspiracies exist and they do not want to be exposed. Let us give four examples of men in our past who understood that conspiracies do exist.

Franklin Delano Roosevelt was purported to have said:

> In politics, nothing happens by accident. If it happens, you can bet it was planned that way.

In other words, there are those who get together to make things happen. Some for good, some for ill. Some openly, some clandestinely.

Abraham Lincoln, in his "House Divided" speech on June 16, 1858 said:

> When we see a lot of framed timbers, different portions of which we know have been gotten out at different times and places and by different workmen — Stephen, Franklin, Roger, and James, for instance — and when we see these timbers joined together, and see they exactly make the frame of a house or mill, all the tenons and mortices exactly fitting, and all the lengths and proportions of the different pieces exactly adapted to their respective places, and not a piece too many or too few — not omitting even the scaffolding — or, if a single piece be lacking, we can see the

place in the frame exactly fitted and prepared to yet bring such a piece in — in such a case, we find it impossible not to believe that Stephen and Franklin and Roger and James all understood one another from the beginning, and all worked upon a common plan or draft drawn up before the first lick was struck.

Lincoln was talking about a political conspiracy or plot on the part of four prominent political figures.

The idea of conspiracies at work was universal when our country began, and there were Founders of our country who were quite concerned about them. In fact, at one point in our early history, John Jay, who became the chief justice of the Supreme Court, was the head of the New York Committee for Detecting and Defeating Conspiracies.

The Founders were aware of the fact that conspiracies exist, and that everything that happens is done because someone wants it that way, and they set about to detect conspiracies as they related to the welfare of our American cause.

There is a conspiracy to eliminate the Second Amendment of our Constitution. Keep in mind that in order for a conspiracy to work, it has to work both sides of the political scale. In other words, the conspirators need to eliminate or neutralize their opposition.

No revolution has been successful without the revolutionaries, working as a conspiracy, having infiltrated the existing government to rot it from within. This was done during the French Revolution and later in China. We are foolish to think it is not being done to our government.

These are the things that those who mean to rule us do not want us to understand.

Let us quote another person of stature, Benjamin Disraeli, former Prime Minister of Great Britain in the mid-1800s, whose statements concerning conspiracy have only been heard by a few:

> The governments of the present day have to deal not merely with other governments, with emperors, kings, and ministers, but also with the secret societies which have everywhere their unscrupulous agents, and can at the last moment upset all the governments' plans.
>
> — Speech at Aylesbury, Great Britain,
> September 10, 1870

Secret societies are often conspiracies, evil being a prerequisite for calling something a "conspiracy."

Another prime minister of Great Britain had something to say about conspiracies, getting much closer to what we are still dealing with today. Winston Churchill wrote in the *Illustrated Sunday Herald* in February 1920:

> From the days of Spartacus-Weishaupt [who founded the secret order of the Illuminati on May 1, 1776] to those of Karl Marx ... this world-wide conspiracy for the overthrow of civilization and the reconstitution of society on the basis of arrested development, of envious malevolence, and impossible equality, has been steadily growing. It played ... a definitely recognizable part in the tragedy of the French Revolution. *It*

*has been the mainspring of every subversive movement during the nineteenth century ....* [Emphasis added.]

Even in the face of these statements by very prominent and important people, there are those who do all that they can to negate any thoughts of a conspiracy at work today.

The words of Churchill tell us the movements of the 19th century, such as Marxism, are the same into the 20th century. He is also saying that Marxism is a conspiracy.

Let us look at another person, J. Edgar Hoover, former head of the FBI, who wrote in *Elks Magazine* in October 1956:

> Yet the individual is handicapped by coming face-to-face with a conspiracy so monstrous he cannot believe it exists. The American mind simply has not come to a realization of the evil which has been introduced into our midst. It rejects even the assumption that human creatures could espouse a philosophy which must ultimately destroy all that is good and decent.

He was talking about communism as a conspiracy.

There can be no question that a conspiracy exists within the United States that has as one of its goals the elimination of our rights, including the Second Amendment.

Keep in mind, again, any conspiracy must work both sides in order to ensure its success. Those who work the "other side" will appear to be against what the extremists are for; however, they will work to move the conspiracy's agenda forward gradually. Usually, they will do all they can to help produce compromises on the road to getting 100 percent of what the conspiracy wants — a step at a time.

Shave off an inch here, and shave off an inch there, and soon there is no longer anything to compromise, they have gained the entire issue. And, it has been done from the inside of the supposed opposition to the revolution.

A very famous study, *Memoirs Illustrating the History of Jacobinism*, was written by a French Catholic priest, Abbe Augustin Barruel, about the French Revolution. Therein he said that the French Revolution would not have been successful if the conspiracy against the French government had not already infiltrated that government: they had no clue that they were even dealing with a conspiracy that had infiltrated their own ranks.

We dwell on the facts of conspiracy because the fight to save the Bill of Rights — and especially the Second Amendment — will be lost if the people defending these rights do not understand what they are up against. This understanding must include the fact that some of those who may appear to be on their side are not. We will show a very blatant example of this in a later chapter.

Finally, although there is much more evidence, let us quote someone who was on the inside and probably Karl Marx's mentor, Frederick Engels. In fact, the two wrote *The Communist Manifesto* together. Engels told the world that the communist organization had two levels, one open and one secret: a conspiracy. We quote a few lines from his article "On the History of the Communist League":

> In 1836 the most extreme ... elements of the secret demo-
> cratic-republican Outlaws' League ... split off and formed
> the new secret League of the Just .... The League was at that
> time actually not much more than the German branch of
> the French secret societies ....

> — Originally published November 12-26,
> 1885 in *Sozialdemokrat: Marx and
> Engels Selected Works*, Volume 3,
> Progress Publishers, Moscow, 1970

This line of organizations produced what became known as the Communist International. Engels also talked about the secret organization within the communist movement in more than one foreword to editions of *The Communist Manifesto* in the late 1800s.

The average communist had no idea he was being directed by a secret organization. Even American leaders in the Communist Party, such as Dr. Bella Dodd and Louis Budenz, who both served on the Central Committee of the American Communist Party, stated that they finally realized that the party was directed by an invisible force.

One important thing we need to clarify before we move on to the next chapter is that what we are talking about is a grab for power. Many people think that it has to do with the money power. While it can include that, the ultimate power is that of government. Money means nothing if you have power.

If you have the ultimate power, money doesn't matter. If you have the money but not the power, it is just paper.

The "great" dictators of the 20th century were all poor. Two of them came up out of the streets: Hitler and Stalin. They didn't need money once they gained power, they had everything at their disposal.

And, how did they gain power? Through a network, an organization, much of it operating in secret.

Now some may say that dealing with a conspiracy is just fiction. Recall the words of Mark Twain: The only difference between reality and fiction is that fiction needs to be credible. Often the truth is incredible.

Let us now examine the aims of the communists and how they relate to our Bill of Rights.

Chapter Two

# THE PLAN OF THOSE WHO OPPOSE AMERICANISM

What do the Marxists have in store for America?

Part of their plan is outlined in *The Communist Manifesto*. You do not have to read all of it, the plan is outlined in ten steps. You would be surprised at what they do *not* say.

However, a few things need to be noticed in the *Manifesto* which give us greater insight into what they have planned and how they mean to change American society.

The *Manifesto* was written by Karl Marx and Frederick Engels as a tool to be used by the communists in the upcoming revolutions in Europe in 1848. It was to be used to help direct the revolutionaries and enlist more adherents into the communist movement.

They stated that their revolution was to be a social revolution, changing society:

> They [the Communists] openly declare that their goals can be attained only by the forcible overthrow of all existing social conditions.

In other words, communism is not so much an armed insurrection as much as it is changing and revolutionizing society. Measures to accomplish this may seem insufficient at first, but those who have studied how others have subverted their governments over the ages know that some measures that make people dependent on government will ultimately garner increasing support, even among the best of libertarians.

Indeed, the ten steps outlined in the *Manifesto* to communize a country deal with issues that change society as much as they change government.

From *The Communist Manifesto*, the ten steps outlining how a communist state will be established are:

These measures will of course be different in different countries.

Nevertheless, in the most advanced countries the following will be pretty generally applicable:

1. Abolition of property in land and application of all rents of land to public purposes.
2. A heavy progressive or graduated income tax.
3. Abolition of all rights of inheritance.
4. Confiscation of the property of all emigrants and rebels.
5. Centralization of credit in the hands of the State, by means of a national bank with State capital and an exclusive monopoly.
6. Centralization of the means of communication and transport in the hands of the State.
7. Extension of factories and instruments of production

owned by the State; the bringing into cultivation of waste-lands, and the improvement of the soil generally in accordance with a common plan.

8. Equal liability of all to work. Establishment of industrial armies, especially for agriculture.

9. Combination of agriculture with manufacturing industries; gradual abolition of the distinction between town and country by a more equable distribution of population over the country.

10. Free education for all children in public schools. Abolition of children's factory labor in its present form. Combination of education with industrial production.

Note that it does not say anything about the confiscation of all guns.

We shall explain why as we go along.

Note that the first, most prominent provision was the elimination of "property in land." The second means to control the people was to tax them and begin to take away even their property in the form of money.

We must make the point that what Marx wanted did not really lead to control of property in land. Property in land is an inanimate object. You cannot control an inanimate object. What he wanted was control over the people. By "controlling" the people, they control the property in land.

This point seems to be lost on the youth who believe that socialism would be a good thing. They support a system that wants to control them, yet rebel against the American system that allows them freedom.

It is a mixed-up way of thinking.

It is interesting that those who stand up and profess to support the American way of life never seem to mention one of the key aspects of Americanism. They more often than not refer erroneously to our system of government as being a democracy. It is a republic, which we shall explain further on.

Let us now tackle the idea which is rarely if ever mentioned as a key component of our system: private property.

It is important to understand this, since it can be used to force people to disarm themselves.

Let us orient ourselves by looking at what our country's Founders had to say about property.

> The moment the idea is admitted into society that property is not as sacred as the laws of God, anarchy and tyranny commence.
>
> — John Adams

What we saw playing out in the streets of America in 2020 is a reflection of the modern attitude that abounds among certain elements of our society and a testament to the truth of Adams' words. Disrespect for property led to the destruction of property in city after city. It did not matter whether it was commercial property, homes, or automobiles, the destruction was the result of a lack of respect for property rights.

In addition, it was not simply the so-called anarchists

torching property who were displaying a lack of respect for property rights, it was also the local governments that did nothing to stop the activity. These local governments displayed a gross disrespect for property and a corresponding disregard for protecting property.

It wasn't so long ago that authorities shut down rioting very quickly. What has happened over the last several years? We will get to the root of the reasons for this as we progress, but first consider this quote from James Madison:

> Government is instituted to protect property of every sort.... This being the end of government.... That is not a just government, nor is property secure under it, where the property which a man has ... is violated by arbitrary seizures of one class of citizens for the service of the rest.

Here we see that President Madison referred to all types of property ("property of every sort"), not just land. So our government was formed to protect property of all kinds. President Madison was known as the Father of the Constitution.

Let us quote John Adams again:

> Property is surely a right of mankind as real as liberty.

The aim of the Marxists is to eliminate landed property and huddle our population into apartment complexes in order to control us better. They have abandoned the idea of spreading people out across the landscape. Various United Nations programs are part of these schemes to cluster us into cities in the name of keeping the land and forests pristine.

As an example of this policy, at the end of World War I, the socialists gained power in Vienna, Austria, and built a huge apartment complex they named after Karl Marx. They then set about organizing every few apartments into communist cells. Soon, a communist revolution began with the apartment complex used as a beehive of agitation unleashed toward the city. As a result, the Austrian army had to begin a cannon barrage against the complex as part of the tactics to quell the rebellion.

Such problems of communist rebellion and so-called anarchy were later used by Hitler as an excuse for his *Anschluss.* Tens of thousands of Austrians waving the swastika welcomed him into Vienna, only to discover that they had jumped from the frying pan into the fire. The confiscation of their firearms played a role in this.

Not owning your own property free from government control, and being placed in a situation in which the government rules where and how you will live, empowers the government to control every other aspect of your life.

# Chapter Three

# TURN IN YOUR PROPERTY

Many Americans believe that they will never turn in their firearms. However, back in the 1930s, many Americans meekly turned in their prized, valuable property out of fear. Let us elaborate.

The Constitution of the United States says that gold and silver are the money of the realm, not paper.

The Continental Congress had experience with paper money, which they issued during the War for Independence. It was a disaster. The money was so inflated, it became worthless. It was not sufficiently backed by gold, allowing the printing presses to roll out massive quantities, which were worthless. They were just paper, after all.

The situation was so bad that a saying cropped up among the people, which lasted into the 20th century: "Not worth a Continental" referred to something that was worthless.

The use of gold and silver as a currency is implied by the Constitution at the federal level, and explicitly mandated at the state government level. Paper money is not authorized anywhere in the Constitution; however, Congress is authorized by the Constitution to "coin money."

The early experience of the Continental Congress with the Continental meant the Founders were very familiar with the idea of paper/printed currency; they had no intention of repeating that mistake by empowering Congress to print paper money.

There is an essential aspect of rare metals that gives the individual freedom. Having gold and silver in one's pocket gives you the opportunity to be free of any entanglements that paper money or "scrip" would entail. The commodities (gold and silver) have value in and of themselves. On the other hand, paper money is supposedly backed by the government or a bank. In the beginning, to get people to trust in paper, it is backed by gold and/or silver, two metals with a high intrinsic value.

Since they were "backed" by the metals, one could take the bills into a bank and exchange them for gold or silver coin.

One can take gold and silver anywhere in the world and be able to use them to live — assuming that the country has not outlawed gold and silver in private hands. Communists immediately confiscate the coins of these metals from the citizens when they take over — usually by going house to house to search for such items (as well as guns). It is not unusual for the resident to then be liquidated if such "contraband" is found.

Paper money is a major step toward government control of the currency, and therefore the individual and business. This step is subtle, but it is there.

Gold and silver may be minted by your government, but foreign minted coinage can also be used. In fact, the Constitution notes this by saying that the government will establish the value of foreign currency:

To coin money, regulate the value thereof, and of foreign coin …

— Article I, Section 8

Nowhere in Section 8 does it give power to Congress to print money. Supposedly Congress got around this lack of power to do so by having the Federal Reserve do it. (The Fed is not part of the government, even though the governors of the Fed are appointed by the executive branch.)

Gold and silver give complete freedom from government to the individual on the financial and economic level. Money based on these rare metals cannot be inflated without massive influxes of new gold or silver into the market. Since these metals are rare and very expensive to mine, this is a very remote possibility.

The amount of gold and silver in a coin determines its value. Paper money of any one nation is generally the same size, and the only thing that makes a difference in its value is the number printed on its face. Without the power of government, paper money would be worth no more than the paper itself, unless backed by rare metals.

Paper money is only as good as the faith people have in it. Once the people understand it is worthless in and of itself, it becomes obsolete. In countries such as Germany in the 1920s, and Venezuela and Zimbabwe in the 2000s, paper became worthless due to a combination of inflation (overprinting the paper currency) and the population's distrust of it.

A study of the price of basic commodities at the beginning of the Federal Reserve in ounces of gold and silver shows the same commodities today, over one hundred years later, cost nearly the same. As opposed to the paper dollar's dramatic loss of value due to inflation, the purchasing power of gold, particularly, and silver, relatively, has stayed the same or done even better. Something that cost x-amount in ounces of gold in 1912, generally costs the same today in ounces of gold, whereas something that cost one paper dollar in 1912 would cost approximately one hundred paper dollars today.

The dollar has suffered a dramatic loss in purchasing power due to a huge increase in the number of dollars in circulation since 1913. Meanwhile, gold and silver have retained their purchasing power due to their scarcity and intrinsic value, and the high cost of mining gold and silver.

Keep in mind that inflation's effects are tied to the goods and services available. If the goods and services expand, over-printing the money may not be noticeable. In the ensuing years since 1913, the growth of goods and services in America (in other words, our economy) has expanded considerably. For inflation to be as bad as it has been, the amount of over-issuance of paper money has to have been phenomenal.

Another aspect of the control of the economy by government is that government does not like any form of the barter system — trading one commodity for another, such as using gold or silver to buy goods. The government finds it very difficult to track such transactions and therefore can't tax them. And if they can't track them, they can't control them.

Totalitarian states do not like the people to hold gold and silver — nor do banking moguls who want to control the economy and the people. Gold and silver are the metals of freedom. Other forms of barter also provide freedom, but paper is a means of control and abusive taxation because it is so traceable.

Just what does this have to do with the Second Amendment? We are dwelling on the property known as gold and silver as an example of what will be done with our guns.

With the advent of the Great Depression at the end of 1929, the country was in deep financial trouble. It was a crisis of monumental proportion. This crisis was used by the government to convince the people that they needed to turn in their gold to the government.

The Constitution says that gold and silver are the money, not paper. The people should have known this due to their understanding of the Constitution. Yet, when the government under Franklin Roosevelt ordered the people in early 1933 to turn in their gold, they dutifully complied.

This was done by an executive order. Try to find "executive order" in the Constitution. It's not there. This power was never delegated to the executive branch, yet the people obeyed.

The people were paid $20.67 per ounce of gold.

The following year, in 1934, the Congress followed up by passing the Gold Reserve Act, which prohibited the private ownership of gold in the United States. This allowed Roosevelt to raise the price of gold by government fiat to

$35 per ounce, thereby raising the price of gold by 69%.

In essence, the Federal government robbed the people, and they stood still for it. After all this, the people reelected Roosevelt three times.

Those who collect gold today say that they would never turn it in, yet the people did so in 1933, when they were supposedly better educated on the rights of the people than they are now.

What if today, using an executive order, the president issued an edict that all people must turn in their guns? How many would comply?

Keep in mind that this edict would be followed up by an act making gun ownership illegal.

In the 1930s the people complied and turned in their gold out of fear due to the economic collapse. What if the people were convinced that chaos in our streets demanded that we give up our guns? How many do you think would then comply?

Don't forget the example of the situation that occurred in St. Louis, where the neighbors got mad at the couple who staved off the mob with their guns. They were obviously fearful of what would happen to them, and blamed the couple who did the right thing.

People marvel today when they realize that Americans turned in their gold in 1933 based not on law, but on presidential fiat. A year later, after the fact, the government passed a law outlawing the private ownership of gold, while at the same time re-evaluating the price of gold to give the government a profit of 69%.

Yet, the Constitution said that gold and silver were the money, not paper. The confiscation of gold was a blatantly unconstitutional act by the Roosevelt administration, dutifully followed by a compliant citizenry.

The parallel between this action and a possible edict to turn in one's guns is striking.

The solution to such a problem we will discuss further on.

# Chapter Four

# DON'T LET A SERIOUS CRISIS GO TO WASTE

In the last chapter regarding turning in their gold, we saw how people could be either programmed out of fear or educated to believe that, in the face of a clear and present danger, the Constitution and Bill of Rights can be ignored.

There have been times that politicians have openly described the tactic of using fear or a crisis to do what they want, though in normal times the people would not stand for it.

Rahm Emanuel, chief of staff for Obama and later the mayor of Chicago, openly explained the tactic at the "2008 Shaping the New Agenda" forum hosted by the *Wall Street Journal*: "You never want a serious crisis to go to waste. What I mean by that, it is an opportunity to do things you think you could not do before."

Hillary Clinton has also alluded to the use of crises to "make things happen," but has not stated it in such a manner for the audience to really understand (except for those aware of the process).

When it comes to gun control, the Democrats seem to have a lock on the initiative. However, although they are not as open about it as the Democrats, there are Republican leaders who also support disarming the people.

The sentiment of the voters in a particular area can determine the "party" a politician runs on. This is a clue to the solution we will offer later.

If the people who want to get elected live in a Republican area, in order to get elected, they run as Republicans — and vice versa for the Democrats.

Political parties and candidates rarely educate their electorates. What they do is take polls to find out what the voters think, and then from these poll results formulate their campaigns accordingly. They may or may not actually believe in the rhetoric they use to garner enough votes to get elected.

They do not educate their constituents to believe in their positions for a few reasons: (1) they fear they may turn people off if they try to change their minds, (2) they simply do not realize the need to do so, or (3) they do not want to take the trouble to do so since it takes a really viable organization to do the job, and it has to be done over a considerable amount of time, between elections, not during an election (then it is too late).

In addition, what tools would they use to educate their voters? Pamphlets, books, speakers, videos, etc.? Who would produce them? How would they disseminate them? It takes time and money to do so.

However, the voters are educated through the schools, media, and local community organizations, which are often nothing more than front groups for social action — meaning socialism. All of these entities promote center-left policies at best.

When a presidential candidate makes statements concerning the disarming of the people and his support of such a move, it means that there is a sizable segment of society that supports such an attitude, or it would be an automatic negation of his campaign because of a lack of support among the voters.

When Joe Biden was running for president, he said that he wanted to sign an executive order banning the importation of "assault weapons" while simultaneously banning their sale. The "gun grabbers" use the term "assault weapons" to make people think they only want to ban combat weapons. Although many private weapons have the silhouette of combat weapons, they are not assault weapons. The real intent of the "assault weapons" ban is the confiscation of *all* the weapons of the people.

Assault weapons are precisely what the men at Lexington and Concord were armed with based on the technology of the time. They may have been muskets, but they were the assault weapons of the time, and the Patriots were not going to let the Redcoats take them.

Biden also wanted to force Americans to either sell their guns to the government under a buyback program or register them with the ATF. The latter may not be gun "confiscation," but it is the first step toward such a program.

The Second Amendment states that the right to keep and bear arms shall not be infringed. This is a powerful statement, because the word "infringed" means a great deal more than what most believe it to mean.

It means that the freedom or right to bear arms cannot be curtailed in any manner, way, shape, or form — period. It means the right cannot be limited or controlled in any way. Registration of firearms is an infringement of that right. It is always the first step toward confiscation, for why else would the government need to know who has firearms and of what type?

A government that fears to have its own people armed, is a government to fear.

Registration can also lead to taxation of the property that is registered. Once that happens, the gun owner is penalized each year for his "ownership" of that property — forever — assuming that his property has not been confiscated. Taxation of property gives tremendous control over the property to the government. If one refuses to pay the tax or cannot afford to pay the tax, what happens then? The property is confiscated one way or another.

In addition to all of the above, there is the danger that people may be prevented from owning guns due to past or current crime as defined by the government — for instance, having been found guilty of a hate crime.

Biden wanted to close the loophole in hate crimes by enacting legislation that would prohibit anyone from owning a gun who has been convicted of a misdemeanor hate crime.

The problem with hate crime is that it can mean whatever the authorities want it to mean at any given time based on the political bent of those in power.

Today, merely voicing opposition to liberal sacred cows such as gay marriage, open borders, and Black Lives Matter will get you accused of "hate speech." How long will it be until it is deemed a "hate crime"?

So *we see the process of limiting the freedom of speech*, which may or may not be done in a peaceful manner, and the loss of this right can be used to curtail gun ownership.

Screaming crowds of people harassing those who do not spew the line they want to have spewed at any given time or location can lead to violent confrontation. Some local authorities condone this, and the innocent bystanders are the ones who are blamed for not submitting to the crowd. When will the local authorities begin to arrest the innocent because they will not bend the knee? This hate crime arrest will then follow them wherever they go.

This is not an outrageous question when one considers that everywhere one goes, he is inundated with slogans that support Marxist initiatives, whether it is on the streets of his metropolitan city, the fields of the National Football League, or the shirts of the National Basketball Association players.

The Germans were programmed to accept the public use by others of the Nazi salute. It wasn't long before it was required by all, punishable by law.

Once the freedoms of speech and thought are stifled, people will be required to violate their beliefs and right-of-center political views will be criminalized. A future government led by a radical would then be authorized to confiscate the guns from law-abiding citizens for the "crime" of holding such views.

When one sees politicians going into the crowd and kneeling before them in submission to the slogan du jour, painting the streets with the slogan, and allowing mobs to become violent in the name of the slogan, then know that the next step could well be the banning of any opposition to the slogan, making it a crime.

This is only two steps away from banning guns from all except those who hold a sufficient rank in the ruling political party, as was done in Nazi Germany and Soviet Russia. The German gun laws forbade private ownership of guns except by Nazi officers.

Only the trusted political operatives need apply.

The use of face masks was recommended during the China virus pandemic even though some medical experts said it was a waste of time. Then it became mandatory indoors at businesses. This led to further edicts in some states to wear them all of the time, indoors, outdoors, at home, whatever. It wasn't long before people started to chastise others who weren't wearing one. What will be the next requirement by edict, not law?

All of these scenarios may seem extreme, yet they have happened elsewhere. Somehow we believe that our people are immune from the herd mentality that others have experienced that has led to oppression. We forget that our ancestors often came from these countries, and we are no different — except to the level that we are educated to understand Americanism.

When we have mobs chanting the latest Marxist slogans in the streets we are only a step away from everyone being ordered to do so.

In communist countries it is not unusual to see massive crowds demonstrating in the streets carrying placards, flags, huge banners, etc., with the slogan of the day and banners or placards with pictures of the Big Brother in that country. The people are required to do so, and those who do not suffer the consequences.

A friend of this author who lived in a communist state related how these demonstrations happened in his country. All of the people were ordered out of work to participate in mass demonstrations, and then people would run to pick up signs, not because they agreed with them but because the first ones there got the little signs and were not burdened with the weight of carrying the big signs.

Another friend related how he was very close to an Iranian while he worked in Iran for several years during the time of the Shah. The man was very pro-Western. Yet when the so-called Islamic revolution took place, my friend, who had returned to the States, saw his friend on television carrying an anti-American sign in a mass demonstration organized by the new Islamic revolution. Fear makes people do things they would not normally do.

Demonstrations are still held in Russia to celebrate the birthdays of Lenin and Stalin, and the anniversary of the

Bolshevik Revolution. The usual hammer and sickle and other communist banners are on display, and demonstrations/parades are held in Red Square, requiring the support of the ruling party in the Kremlin. Since the demonstrations are officially sanctioned, it is obvious that the collapse of communism in Russia is a sham. The same totalitarians rule, they just call themselves democrats.

To further illustrate that these demonstrations are sanctioned and even posed, consider that for decades — from the time of communism up through "democracy" — Russian authorities have released photographs of parades in Moscow and their participants for the use of the foreign press, and that they have consistently provided photos of the same woman carrying pictures of Lenin and Stalin.

Out of the crowd of thousands participating in each event, the official photographer always seems to "pick" this same woman. (Although the woman clearly and visibly ages over the years, the average American reader has never seemed to notice this. Certainly the foreign press have not — or they have actually been working for the communists while representing the Western news services. The journalists simply take what is issued to them by the Russian authorities and regurgitate it to their bosses in New York.)

The odds of this woman being photographed year after year are astronomical, clearly indicating that these are posed events.

The point is that totalitarian authorities hold sway over the masses, and we see this starting to be a problem in some areas of our country through intimidation and violence. Opposition is portrayed as systemic racism, white supremacy, etc., only a step away from hate crime in the eyes of the Fake News and some politicians.

In such a manner, the average American who opposes the breakdown of law and order can be prevented from being able to ever own a gun. The same goes for a person who simply advocates the private ownership of guns — obviously a "hater" according to some politicians and the mass media.

So we see again where the loss of freedom of speech can be turned into an excuse to take away one's right to gun ownership.

# Chapter Five

# OPEN BORDERS

The problems that we have seen along our borders have played into the hands of those who want to disarm Americans.

Generally speaking, there is a certain level of violence existing in our communities due to the criminals and weapons that have crossed into America illegally. This then creates a cry from the people to solve the problem of crime, especially crime involving a gun.

This problem has obvious and not-so-obvious aspects.

One of the most obvious is the organizing of many of these illegal aliens into gangs that harass and control ethnic areas of our cities, with a certain amount of slop-over into the suburbs.

We have all seen news programs documenting the criminal behavior, murder, and mayhem by criminal aliens. These aliens never seem to be expelled from our country or placed in prison until they have become a serious problem for everyone and there is finally a hue and cry over these particular individuals. However, there is rarely any outcry against the illegal criminal element in general in cities around the country — especially sanctuary cities.

In the countries south of our border, it is not unusual to see that the cartels are stronger than the local police units and can shoot their way out of many situations, leaving dead police on the streets.

Some Mexican states, for example, are actually controlled by cartels rather than the Mexican government. Kidnapping of both foreigners and native Mexicans is a national pastime in some areas.

An American lady related to me how she had to take precautions with her sister when she went to Mexico to retrieve the body of her husband, who had died there. The hotel had to rent a private car and driver so that she would not be noticed. Kidnapping was such a problem that a foreigner riding around in a taxicab could be noticed and targeted in that area.

The problem with cartels in America involving aliens is one thing, but what has also been happening and receiving little attention is the smuggling of weapons into the United States. We have seen photos of three separate caches of arms that have been interdicted at the border that amount to company-grade infantry weapons, including rocket launchers, grenades, machine guns, assault rifles, and ammunition, each in a quantity capable of arming an infantry company. No one seems to know where these arms are destined to go. In one case, an armored SUV was captured as well. Either the smugglers get away before being captured along with the weapons, or they don't reveal the destination of these arms.

If the federal government knows where they are destined to go, they are not talking, either.

If the amount of these weapons being interdicted at our borders is at the same level as the amount of drugs being caught, then a lot of weapons are making their way into our country. For what purpose?

An obvious answer is to supply cartels forming within our borders. Another is to sell them to criminals to get around gun laws.

One's imagination can run wild just thinking about what the weapons are for.

One thought is, when will the Marxist demonstrators in the streets become armed? One shudders to think of the harm that can be done before the police arrive, even if the police are allowed to do their job. They can be outgunned.

These thoughts would have been outrageous a few years ago. Now, who knows?

In any case, whatever these weapons are to be used for, it will mean that the people will demand that something be done to get them off of the streets. This could well be a catalyst for a rise in the demand to get rid of all firearms.

And, of course, if this were done, the only people who would have weapons would be the criminals and the government — and the revolutionaries.

We do not know whether this will happen or not, we are only offering several scenarios that could be used for disarming the people and destroying the Second Amendment.

Another aspect of smuggling is that the Chinese have been smuggling people into the United States for some time, in addition to the hundreds of thousands of students and others on visas. They have come in shipping containers and been led across our southern border by coyotes — professional guides — dozens at a time. Those crossing into America from the south are usually below the age of 30 — destination unknown. Their purpose of coming in an organized fashion is also not known.

Since the Chinese have control over some of our ports, the lack of sufficient inspection of containers is very troubling, regardless of what they contain. Arms perhaps? Who knows.*

Another aspect of the pressure that could come to disarm everyone is the rise in crime in some of our major cities.

It is obvious that some of our local leaders are either dedicated Marxists or incredibly stupid in how they have dealt with rioting and crime on the streets.

Everyone who pays any attention to the news knows that the rise in crime, especially as it relates to shooting people, is worse than it is in Afghanistan. Major cities have shootings in the thousands per year, with the number of people killed in the hundreds.

The attacks of the Taliban rarely result in the number of deaths occurring on the streets of Chicago on any given weekend, yet they gather more headlines than the problems in Chicago, or New York, or wherever. It is not unusual that 50 people are shot in a weekend in Chicago.

More police are shot and killed in our cities than all of the American troops deployed in the Middle East in supposed combat zones.

At some point, the pressure to disarm the criminals will

---

* For a look at the problem of Chinese infiltration, see *China: The Deep State's Trojan Horse in America*. Available at ShopJBS.org.

mean the disarming of everyone. After all, there would not be a declaration that only criminals line up at their local police station to turn in their weapons; everyone would be told to do so.

Riots and looting sprees are not stopped in many of the major cities, allowing property to be stolen or burned to the ground. The crime may be stopped after a couple of days due to public pressure, but it is known that some mayors have ordered their police departments to stand down and allow the chaos to continue in the name of not wanting to stop "demonstrations" in support of some cause that the city officials obviously agree with.

In the case of Seattle in 2020, the mayor even called the taking over of a major section of Seattle by Marxist agitators and terrorists a "Summer of Love."

Often the rioters were allowed get a good head of steam, and in some cases they were allowed to go on for months. In other cases, they were only curtailed for a time once the rioters visited the homes of the mayors in the suburbs and scared the mayor and family out of their wits. The rioters apparently hadn't gotten the word who their friends were.

Then the mayors got "religion." They made the police guard their homes and property, but not the homes of private citizens. Some are more equal than others.

The problem is one of property rights. Our country was founded on the right of private property. To establish this, and to show how important this was to our Founders, let us again quote some of them in this regard:

> The moment the idea is admitted into society that property is not as sacred as the laws of God, anarchy and tyranny commence.
>
> — John Adams

> Government is instituted to protect property of every sort …. This being the end of government … .That is not a just government, nor is property secure under it, where property which a man has … is violated by arbitrary seizures of one class of citizens for the service of the rest.
>
> — James Madison

As we commented earlier, President Madison is referring to all types of property (property of every sort). So our government was formed to protect property — property of all kinds.

Let us quote John Adams again:

> Property is surely a right of mankind as real as liberty.

In addition, property rights are included in the Bill of Rights twice.

The Fourth Amendment states: "The right of the people to be secure in their person, house, papers, and effects, against unreasonable searches and seizures, shall not be violated," etc.

The Fifth Amendment states that a person can "not be deprived of life, liberty, or property, without due process of law: nor shall private property be taken for public use without just compensation."

The people understood their rights, property and otherwise, and wanted to make sure that they were proclaimed and protected in the Constitution.

Over time many of these rights have been violated, often without the vast majority of the people realizing it; in some cases, out of ignorance, some people have even supported such violations. This violation of property rights has been carried out in concerted attacks against property of all sorts and by "educating" the people into ignorance.

What is property?

The answer is that it is everything necessary for the survival of man in the broadest sense. Not only for survival, but for his pleasure as well. It does not mean another person, male or female, is property.

The Judeo-Christian view is that God put everything on Earth for the benefit of man. It is man's property, under the authority of God, in other words. With it, of course, came the responsibility to husband the land, animals, etc. America was founded on this Judeo-Christian view.

Property can be land, the animals and plants on that land, personal property, inventory, machinery, buildings, goods, even one's services.

And, of course, his arms.

As the respect for property rights deteriorates, the public attitude toward the right to keep and bear arms is also affected.

As an example: What happens to you if you are a renter and you do not pay your rent? You are evicted. What if you are a property owner and do not pay your taxes? You are evicted. What is the difference? You realize that you do not "own" your property in the truest sense.

Now, what if a tax were imposed on your guns and you didn't pay it?

The rights of property have a direct bearing on the right to keep and bear arms.

We will now look at how foreign treaties can have a bearing on the Second Amendment.

# Chapter Six

# FOREIGN ENTANGLEMENTS

How in the world could foreign treaties have a bearing on the Second Amendment?

The answer to that lies in the thousands of pages that come after the innocuous title on a treaty or any international agreement. The title is designed to make people support whatever it is that is in the body of the agreement, though it often has nothing to do with what the core of the treaty is all about.

It is rare that people read the treaties, even those who sign them or those who ratify them in the Congress. This is difficult to do when some are 2,000 or even 3,000 pages long by the time they are ratified. Often, the ratification process is planned so that Congress doesn't have time to read an agreement, with sometimes only a matter of hours from release to vote. Then, too, the language of the treaties is not always clear, since they are written in "legalese," which only lawyers and the astute can understand.

One of the worst agreements the United States has ever entered into is the United Nations Charter. With this agreement, we lost a great deal of our sovereignty and the freedoms that the American people enjoyed, even though many of the regulations may not yet rest heavily on our shoulders, or at least not to the extent that they have been noticed by the average American.

In some instances the regulations being imposed on the American people are noticed, but not always as coming from the UN — they are imposed by various levels of American government to comply with UN edicts. Most of these regulations are being imposed in the Western states by violating property rights in the name of the environment.

The most obvious aim of the United Nations is the complete disarming of civilians and armies. Most people think that the UN was established to bring about universal peace. It was actually established to bring about a one-world government.

Let us set the stage for considering whether a world government is desirable by remembering the adage that the British Lord Acton coined: Power tends to corrupt and absolute power corrupts absolutely.

This idea, before being coined by Lord Acton, was always on the mind of our Founders. They knew the nature of man, and especially that of government. They knew that government always accumulates power to the detriment of its own people. It is like night following day.

As a result, they formulated a Constitution in order to curtail this tendency of government. They limited the government and spelled out precisely what powers the government was to have. Many people were still not satisfied, and this led to the Bill of Rights, the first ten amendments to the Constitution, further defining our rights and further curtailing what the government was allowed to do — and stating that if the government didn't comply with the rules, the states and/or the people were not to follow it.

As an example of what is wrong with the United Nations, consider how the Charter of the UN and its Universal Declaration of Human Rights are totally opposite to our system of government.

We declare that our rights come from God; the UN declares that they come from government. We declare that government does not have the right to pass laws in violation of these rights; the UN declares that government has the right to pass laws to limit our freedoms. This is a completely different idea — and totalitarian.

As part of the problem, every international agreement we have entered into has come under the jurisdiction of the UN. Some of the treaties and agreements mention this fact right up front, as in the case of NATO, but others bury it deep in the agreement.

These things are a serious problem when it comes to our right to keep and bear arms.

Our forefathers understood the problems that would ensue if we got tangled up with foreign nations, that the American people would lose their independence and the freedom to make their own decisions — that we would come under the control of foreign interests, and ultimately their domination.

> It is our policy to steer clear of permanent alliances with any portion of the foreign world … .
>
> — George Washington, 1796

> Commerce with all nations, alliance with none, should be our motto.
>
> — Thomas Jefferson, 1799

> I deem (one of) the essential principles of our government (to be) peace, commerce, and honest friendship with all nations, entangling alliances with none.
>
> — Thomas Jefferson, 1801

In 1952, John Foster Dulles addressed a meeting of the American Bar Association in Louisville, Kentucky, saying this:

> Treaties make international law and they also make domestic law. Under our Constitution, treaties become the supreme law of the land .... Treaties, for example, can take powers away from the Congress and give them to the President; they can take powers from the states and give them to the federal government or to some international body, and they can cut across the rights given to the people by their constitutional Bill of Rights.

Every thought in this quote is erroneous and against the idea and spirit of the Constitution and Bill of Rights.

John Foster Dulles was named secretary of state by Dwight David Eisenhower shortly after this speech was given. He was a founder of the Council on Foreign Relations (CFR), and Eisenhower was a member. The CFR is a globalist organization whose members are dedicated more to the idea of a New World Order than to the United

States. They comprise a very important part of what has become known as the Deep State.*

Contrast Dulles' words with those of our Founders, who said:

> A treaty cannot be made which alters the Constitution of the country, or which infringes any express exceptions to the power of the Constitution of the United States.
>
> — Alexander Hamilton, 1795

> The only constitutional exception to the power of making treaties is that it shall not change the Constitution…. On natural principles, a treaty which should manifestly betray or sacrifice primary interests of the state would be null.
>
> — Alexander Hamilton, 1796

> I say the same as to the opinion of those who consider the grant of the treaty-making power as boundless. If it is, then we have no Constitution.
>
> — Thomas Jefferson, 1803

Yet, according to a prime shaker in the founding of the CFR, John Foster Dulles, treaties can supersede the Constitution.

Let us analyze a little closer the words of Dulles, since they permeate the thinking of so many in government to-

---

* For a comprehensive look at the Council on Foreign Relations, see *In the Shadows of the Deep State*, or *Deep State: The Invisible Government Behind the Scenes*, both available from ShopJBS.org. Many of the problems we have concerning the movement toward an internationalist foreign policy and Marxism at home are attributable to the CFR.

day and in the membership of the CFR.

The supreme law of the land is the Constitution, not treaties. If treaties take powers away from Congress, then the Constitution becomes amended in an unconstitutional manner. However, Dulles' last words are the most dangerous: "they can cut across the rights given to the people by their constitutional Bill of Rights."

First of all, our rights were not given to us by the Bill of Rights. We derive our rights from God. The Bill of Rights and the Constitution only protect our rights. Most governments bestow rights on the people — this is the opposite of the philosophy on which our country was founded.

Secondly, what we see in Dulles' remarks is the idea that we can even lose our rights due to treaties. This is an audacious and dangerous idea.

Essentially, such thinking by Dulles amounts to treason against everything our system stands for. But it is the thinking of the Council on Foreign Relations and too much of our State Department today.

At the conclusion of Dulles' remarks, the attorneys at the ABA stood and applauded.

Books have been written which document the problems with the UN and how the UN is influencing the actions of our own government.* However, we will confine ourselves to the Second Amendment and our ability to defend our-

---

* Several books have been written highly critical of the United Nations and exposing what the UN has been doing to subvert the American system and rule the planet. Some are *The United Nations: Unity Through Tyranny,* by Arthur R. Thompson;

selves as citizens and a country.

Once the UN was formed, the United States named ambassadors to the United Nations. In the ensuing years, 38 people have been named to this position, and 60 percent have been members of the CFR. They served under 13 presidents, of whom 54 percent were members of the CFR. This does not include UN ambassadors who belonged to other organizations that promoted some aspect of globalism over American independence.

In other words, our representatives to the UN who were members of the CFR wanted a one-world government to the detriment of the independence of the United States. If they served under a president who was also a member of the CFR, then this explains why there was little pushback against the UN assuming more and more control over American foreign policy and internal policies, and why such documents as *Freedom From War: The United States Program for General and Complete Disarmament in a Peaceful World*, planning to turn our armed forces over to the UN, would become the official policy of the U.S. government — at the height of the Cold War!

Nearly 60 years later, this document is still in force, augmented by additional documents pertaining to our

---

*Inside the United Nations: A Critical Look at the UN*, by Steve Bonta; and *Global Tyranny ... Step by Step: The United Nations and the Emerging New World Order* and *The United Nations Exposed*, both written by William F. Jasper. They are available at ShopJBS.org.

disarmament. The government agency which oversaw the subject, the United States Arms Control and Disarmament Agency, was established in 1961 and was abolished in 1999. It was last headed by John D. Holum, a member of the CFR, from 1993-99. Its functions were absorbed into the Department of State in 1999.

This is the reason many presidents have allowed our military to deteriorate, necessitating presidents such as Reagan and Trump to beef them up once again.

What about a UN army? What would it be like?

A clue rests in those who have been appointed UN Under-Secretary-General for Political and Security Council Affairs. This was the office under which the UN army would have been enforced. From the founding of the UN in 1945 until 1992, 14 people held this post; all were communists and all but one came from the Soviet Union.

After the so-called collapse of communism in the Soviet Union, the image of this office changed. Changes were made until in 2019 the responsibilities were moved to the Department of Political and Peacebuilding Affairs. Its role, however, never changed, just its public image.

The last three heads of the agencies that carried out this responsibility have been Americans — of a particular stripe. Two are members of the CFR, while the third came out of the Brookings Institution, which is run by members of the CFR.

We are always told that politicians make mistakes. We believe them until we run into documents such as *Freedom*

*From War* and note the amazing coincidences of who runs the disarmament agencies of the UN. If there is a plan, then there is a group of people who have put together the plan and implemented it out of sight of the general public. Some would call it a conspiracy.

There are two other facts concerning the United Nations we need to take note of before we see the UN's attitude about civilians owning firearms.

One, Chinese communists occupy more chairs of UN agencies than any other country. This does not count other communists who occupy the chairs of UN agencies. Two, the leaders of the UN General Assembly have all been either communists or militant socialists — every one of them, starting with Alger Hiss, the Soviet American spy, and ending up with Antonio Guterres, a Portuguese communist.

When it comes to world government, the United Nations has a plan to disarm every individual on Earth.

One need not look any further than the large statue that exists on the plaza just outside the UN building in New York to get an idea of what they have in store. It is a large replica of a .357 caliber Magnum revolver that has a twisted barrel, making it inoperative. It is symbolic of the desire of the UN to eliminate all private firearms, not just the accouterments of war.

The title of the sculpture is "The Knotted Gun." It was donated to the UN by Luxembourg in 1988. There are 30 copies of the statue around the world, but this is the original. In a similar vein, the USSR donated a "Let Us Beat Our

Swords Into Ploughshares" statue to the UN back in 1959.

There never was a plan by the rioters in the streets to tear down these statues, as they were doing to American icons of our past in city after city.

Modern American education is doing an inadequate job of teaching the American system and the reasons for our system. You can imagine the problems that would ensue if a world government was made up of people who do not understand any aspect of what makes the American system work.

While it may be a growing problem in America, it is the problem with the United Nations already.

Just one example of this is the difference between the American Bill of Rights and the United Nations International Covenant on Civil and Political Rights. These supposedly are the same thing, but they are quite different.

The Bill of Rights states:

> Amendment I: Congress shall make no law respecting an establishment of religion, or prohibiting the free exercise thereof; or abridging the freedom of speech or of the press; or the right of the people peacefully to assemble, and to petition the Government for a redress of grievances.

Congress shall make no law — period. This also implies that government cannot limit these rights in case of an emergency. Once that process starts, it is a slippery slope.

The United Nations International Covenant, Article 18 states:

> Everyone shall have the right to freedom of thought, conscience and religion.

## It goes on to state:

> Freedom to manifest one's religion or beliefs may be subject only to such limitations as are prescribed by law.

This is very different from the idea that government cannot pass a law limiting our rights, as stated in the Bill of Rights. In other words, according to the UN, you have the right to freedom of religion or thought as long as some government doesn't pass a law against it.

Again, Article 19 of the UN covenant states:

> Everyone shall have the right to hold opinions without interference.

## Then it states:

> The exercise of the rights provided for in … this article carries with it special duties and responsibilities. It may therefore be subject to certain restrictions, but these shall only be such as are provided by law and are necessary.

Again, very different from the spirit of the Bill of Rights, which is that government cannot regulate opinions or speech — period.

The UN covenant goes on to limit the freedom of assembly and association with others — as prescribed by law — if necessary. The slippery slope is built right into the UN's statement of rights.

They do not even mention ownership of guns. And if they did, they would also have put in the proviso "as prescribed by law and are necessary." It is very interesting that they omit any reference to private ownership of guns. If they said anything they would be condemned for their position, so they ignore it hoping people will not notice.

Actually, by not mentioning it, they are saying that it isn't a right, whether it is curtailed or not.

What we have here is that the UN's idea of freedom is the exact opposite of freedom as expressed in the Bill of Rights.

Americans do not realize just how different our form of government is compared to the rest of the world, and certainly to the UN.

The United Nations International Covenant on Civil and Political Rights was ratified by the U.S. Senate on April 2, 1992 with only one dissenting voice, demonstrating just how precarious our rights are in light of the Swamp in Washington.

Before leaving the subject of the United Nations, we should look at other aspects of our system vs. the UN's and other countries' in general.

Most of the communists' goals are delineated in *The Communist Manifesto*. Of the two main goals, one is mentioned openly: unification of the world into a single government to be ruled by the communist parties united.

The second main goal, though not explicitly stated, is to eliminate God from public life and replace Him with the state.

No totalitarian government tolerates a religion that places God above the state. The use of the schools in dictatorships to indoctrinate the youth into literally worshiping the Big Brother leader has been done over and over again, such as in Germany with Hitler, Russia with Stalin, China with Mao, etc.

The state wants nothing to come between the government and the people as to whom they will obey. They have been doing it from the time of the Roman emperors to today. To the Christians, Rome basically said, "Worship the state's gods or die."

The Declaration of Independence provides a protective shield between us and the goals of the communists and one-worlders. It states that our rights come from God and that we are independent from the rest of the world. Is it any wonder that the Declaration is no longer taught in today's schools as to the full meaning and spirit of the document?

In 2020 the teachers refused to go back to school due to the China virus pandemic and several other Leftist initiatives from state to state. It is not surprising that students are turned out that are rebels against the American system. A little over ten years ago, the National Education Association (NEA) urged its teachers to read *Rules for Radicals* by Saul Alinsky. Alinsky was a Marxist radical who helped organize community action organizations that promoted

Marxism. This book by Alinsky was dedicated to Lucifer! If you cannot believe this, obtain a copy and look for yourself. Within a few years, the NEA withdrew its endorsement of Alinsky's book.

What do you think they teach about the Bill of Rights? In the 1970s, a school district in the so-called conservative state of Idaho taught this (we will only quote two), as if it were the true wording of the amendments:

> Amendment II: The people have the right to keep and bear arms, but Congress may regulate private weapons.

> Amendment IV: People or their homes or other belongings cannot be searched or seized without good cause.

It has only gotten worse in many instances. Is it any wonder the students do not have a clue about the Bill of Rights?

Parents have to start paying attention to what their children are being taught.

What most people are not aware of is that the teachers unions in America are members of the UN-controlled Education International (EI), started by a leader in the American Socialist Party, Albert Shanker (since deceased). EI was formed out of the so-called free-world unions and the former communist unions that were behind the Iron Curtain. On the collapse of communism, the communist teachers unions did not change in substance, but in name only.

None of the teachers who taught in the communist-controlled countries quit being communists. They simply called themselves democrats.

The United Nations Educational, Scientific and Cultural Organization, UNESCO, has a tremendous influence on American education. At one time, Ronald Reagan withdrew us from the organization due to the adverse effect it was having on the education of our youth. After Reagan, though, we once again joined UNESCO.

There were increasing cries to leave the organization again as a result of its efforts to impose Common Core education on American students and a common curriculum for the entire world, eliminating our American heritage and foundational documents from American schools. Their aim is to have every student on Earth taught the same things on the same day all around the world.*

President Trump finally pulled us out of UNESCO again when he became president.

The curricula being taught today as a result of Common Core relative to our right to keep and bear arms is terrible. The backlash by parents once they saw what was being taught made their school districts supposedly revert back to the systems taught before Common Core, but in reality they simply changed the name from Common Core to something else.

Parents need to be vigilant. The real solution is to put your children into private education and/or home schooling.

Now we have shown you how the abrogation of even more rights can be used to limit the people on an interna-

---

* The full story of Common Core can be researched by searching for "freedomproject" "common core."

tional scale and can be used to limit gun ownership. But the final goal of the UN remains to be exposed.

We have a system of local police, only beholden to local citizens. Totalitarian governments have national police forces, beholden to the state. Our local system came under increased attack with efforts to nationalize the police in the name of the riots of 2020. Several organizations even attempted to have the UN intervene in the riots and the reasons behind the riots — instigating investigations of local governments in the process.

The United States is under enormous pressure to move control of its police from the local level to the national level. This would be followed by international standards, and finally international control.

The UN would certainly be able to implement its long-standing goal of civilian disarmament if they had control of our local police, either directly or through international standards. As an example of UN thinking about this, on August 18, 2014, in the wake of protests in Ferguson, Missouri, following the fatal shooting of Michael Brown, United Nations Secretary-General Ban Ki-moon released a statement demanding that local (American) law enforcement adhere to "international standards."

On the UN website there are many articles advocating the confiscation of private firearms, varying from speculation to recommendations for all private guns to be confiscated. And, as Article 2 of the UN's Arms Trade Treaty (approved by the UN General Assembly in 2013, signed by the U.S. in 2013, but not yet ratified by the U.S. Senate) reveals, the UN's international standards include a prohibition on civilians' right to own, buy, sell, trade, or transfer all means of armed resistance, including handguns.*

This says it all.

---

* As reported by Joe Wolverton in "Kerry Signs UN Arms Trade Treaty — Civilian Disarmament Advancing" posted on September 25, 2013 at TheNewAmerican.com.

# Chapter Seven

# SAVE OUR DEMOCRACY

No matter where one turns, the word "democracy" is used to describe our system of government.

This is even true of the conservative pundits whom patriotic Americans watch or listen to every day. One well-known conservative news network even referred to their coverage of the elections as "Democracy 2020."

When in school in the early 1950s, we were told that there was no difference in which word you used to describe our system of government, republic or democracy. The same civics teacher in our school even said that communism wasn't really bad, it's just that bad people have tried to implement it.

We wish we could go back and ask for sufficient time to describe for our fellow students what the differences are and their importance to the freedom and independence of the American people, as well as the fact that communism is bad no matter who tries to implement it.

In *The Communist Manifesto*, Marx and Engels state that they want to win the battle for democracy. People who read that believe that the communists are lying. They are not. They want a democracy on the road to a dictatorship of the proletariat.

Let us explain how this relates to the right to keep and

bear arms.

Is the United States a democracy? Ask anyone what type of government we have and most will answer, "democracy." After all, the majority decide one way or the other at the ballot box — right?

Yet we stand and pledge allegiance to the flag and to the *Republic* for which it stands. We do not say for the *democracy* for which it stands.

Many people think that those who do not stand for the flag salute do so out of a lack of patriotism; that is only partially true. The vast majority of people do not realize that those who want to change our system do not want anyone to be reminded that this is a republic, not a democracy — hence the objection to the flag salute.

Through the years, the Marxists have ingrained into the American psyche support for the system of democracy. The schools, particularly, have left out the differences between a republic and a democracy.

Basically, the difference is that democracy is majority rule. A republic is a representative system based on inviolate law. Yes, the people vote, but they are bound by law, not whim. There are things for which they cannot vote.

Is voting to take property or guns away from one group and give them to another stealing? Or simply confiscating property or guns? If it is stealing, even if made legal, then it is wrong. No majority changes this fact.

Is it proper to promote the belief that a minority is inferior and should have more draconian regulations placed on them as a result? Even to the point of eliminating them from the population? Of course not, yet Germany, an educated society, did it in the 1930s to the Jews and China does it today to its minority populations.

So, again, there are actions which should not even be voted on; they are already immoral or illegal if done by individuals. Just because the majority believes in taking these actions does not make them legal or moral. Sometimes the issues are more subtle than the examples we have given. When they are, they will always lead to things which are more overt and obvious, but too late.

The latter is what is happening today with the right of gun ownership, which is being snipped away a little at a time with subtle limitations that are leading ultimately to full gun control and confiscation. And, it is being done in the name of the people, moving more and more people toward advocating a change in, and then the elimination of, the Second Amendment.

A pure democracy involves the people at every turn. It is by mass vote. The people are directly involved in all decisions by mass vote. Without laws "set in stone," it leads to mobocracy. Whoever sways the mob rules, and that will always be the superior organization and/or the media. If a secret combination controls both, the results are quickly disastrous. This is the direction of those who desire to mislead the people, and it leads to a dictatorship of the proletariat, the first step in the Marxist program as outlined in *The Communist Manifesto*.

Even if the transition is without violence, once the majority finds out that they can tax the minority for whatever purpose, they will, and this destroys the economic system and the right to property, and along the way the right to gun ownership. Here too the superior organization and/or media will use this propensity of the "have-nots" to covet to determine the course of the nation.

In a real democracy, freedom dies in favor of the majority. There are no protections for the rights of the minorities. The majority can do whatever they like to the minorities, whether the minorities are an economic status, race, or religion.

Recall that many times in the 20th century minorities were used, abused, and even killed. We have given two examples, Germany and China, but this process has continued into the 21st century in the Mideast, Southeast Asia, and elsewhere. Minorities live in fear in these areas every day, especially over differences in religion and race.

In Rwanda, the majority Hutus slaughtered the Tutsis. In Southeast Asia, Rohingya Muslims have flooded into Bangladesh from Myanmar (formerly Burma) due to the majority Buddhists killing them and burning their homes. In country after country in the Middle East, majority sects of Muslims have killed minority sects of Muslims along with Christians and Jews over the past 30 years.

Majority rule is not a good principle if the people are not checked by laws which are inviolate and sustained by an informed people.

In such an atmosphere as described above, one certainly

would like to be armed. But it would not mean a thing if your neighbors were not armed as well, to defend not only a home but a city.

A democracy is unstable because of all of the reasons stated above: the majority will vote themselves some advantage to the detriment of the minority(ies).

Marx and Engels recognized the instability of a democracy, and they also recognized the advantages of propagandizing for democracy in the name of the people. Never believe that their use of the term was phony. The Marxists really do want democracy as the first step toward a totalitarian government. Because of its instability, the Marxists can manipulate a democracy into a communist party-led government

This does not mean that everyone who calls themselves Democrat or Republican holds the core beliefs of the leadership of any political party. The grassroots of both major political parties have always been misused by their leaders, and policies instituted by the leadership have not always been what the people supported or elected them to do. The leaders have gotten away with it because people tend to listen to the rhetoric rather than look at the fruit of the action of their leaders, or the actions have been sold as a compromise between two opposing forces. Usually, the fix is in at the top and the rest is show business.

Reiterating, Marx and Engels said in *The Communist Manifesto*: "The first step in the revolution of the working class is to raise the proletariat to the position of ruling class to win the battle of democracy."

The battle of democracy is to be the first step in the revolution. It is interesting that the mob enlisted by the communists never ask what the next steps are.

Note also that *they* are to be the *ruling class* — so much for the idea of a democracy for all the people.

The revolution of the communists is supposed to eliminate the ruling class, yet they only want to substitute who the ruling class will be. It won't be the people. It will be those who have manipulated the people.

Once the republic is destroyed through democracy, the next step in the revolution is to use the majority to eliminate all opposition to communism, generally by mob action. Enemies of the conspiracy will be first isolated and then executed. It has happened time and time again when communists have taken control of a country.

Once the effective opposition to the conspiracy is eliminated, the third step — a dictatorship — is established over everyone, including the mob: a so-called dictatorship of the proletariat.

And, it is all done by a secret organization who knows what it is doing and where it wants to take the people. Engels said so himself on more than one occasion, in at least two forewords to editions of the *Manifesto* and elsewhere.

Much of this has been purged from the record so the innocent do not realize what is going on. Our country's Founders knew history, however, and were fearful of the possibility of such machinations. They were also fearful of conspiracies.

The idea of conspiracies at work was a universal idea when

our country began, and the Founders of our country were quite concerned about them. We have already used the example of John Jay chairing a committee to detect conspiracies.

It is interesting that as the country comes under the sway of those who want more government, the media and those in authority attack people who believe in conspiracies.

For all the above reasons and more, John Adams in a letter to John Taylor in 1814 said this:

> Democracy never lasts long. It soon wastes, exhausts and murders itself. There never was a democracy yet, that did not commit suicide.

The great writer and philosopher G. K. Chesterton understood why there was a movement toward democracy in the world. He said:

> You can never have a revolution in order to establish a democracy. You must have a democracy in order to have a revolution.

A republic is the rule of law, usually with a representative system whereby the citizens elect their local representatives, and then each body so elected in turn elects the representatives to the next level of government. All of this is done based on a set of laws that are inviolate.

Rome had a set of laws that made it a republic for centuries, until democracy set in. Democracy led to the violation of those laws which had formed the foundation of the republic. Democracy ultimately led to the tyrannical emperors and their excesses over all of the people (except those employed to enforce the edicts of the government — they lived rather well).

The Constitution of the United States was established to limit the government. In it, you will not find the word "democracy." Nor will you find that word in any of the fifty state constitutions. What you will find is that the federal Constitution mandates that all states have a republican system of government: republics.

Yet we have moved a great deal away from the republican system in practice due to over a century of education and subversion by the Marxists within our country.

The change from inviolate law can only lead to the point where gun ownership becomes illegal. Our republican system with its checks and balances, and its inviolate laws, must be understood and maintained.*

---

* The best references for the difference between a republic and a democracy are the DVD *Overview of America*; the booklet *Republics and Democracies* by Robert Welch; and *Back to the Republic* by Harry F. Atwood, Laird & Lee, Inc. Publishers, Chicago, 1918. The latter is particularly recommended, but the former two items are easy to procure at www.ShopJBS.org.

# Chapter Eight

# CHANGES IN THE REPUBLIC

The concerted pressure on, and education of, the people by the organized Marxists started to take its toll at the turn of the 20th century.

Influenced by both the American Marxists and the flood of immigrants who were also imbued with Marxism, the American people started to think our country was a democracy. The Europeans who came to America after the revolutions of 1848-49 were mostly those who supported socialism — or at least had no appreciation for the virtues of the American system — as the revolutions were led by either communists or socialists with a large following among the European people.

Our history books refer to them as revolutions for democracy, which was true, except they never delineate the problems with democracy and that *The Communist Manifesto* called for democracy.

The buildup in the minds of too many Americans to support democracy was done without them realizing what they were supporting. In their minds it was simply majority rule.

By 1917, we even went to war to "Save Democracy."

Also by 1917, we had already changed our system of government drastically.

How did these changes affect the people's outlook on

the Bill of Rights, which includes the Second Amendment? We shall see.

The changes that were made included two amendments to the Constitution, the Sixteenth and Seventeenth, as well as the establishment of the Federal Reserve Bank.

As a result of these changes, two steps from *The Communist Manifesto* outlining how to make over a country into a communist one were initiated: step two, the income tax, and step five, a central bank.

The income tax was initiated during the Civil War by the federal government, and it went generally unchallenged due to the emergency and need for funding the war. After the war it was phased out, but there was an attempt to reimpose it shortly thereafter. At this time the Supreme Court ruled that the tax was unconstitutional.

The Constitution did not allow for the direct taxation of the people. The method for funding the federal government was a system of tariffs and excise taxes primarily, and if federal spending exceeded the amount of taxes thus collected, the states were billed for the overage proportionally based on each state's population.

At this time, the Congress represented two entities: the people and the state governments. While the people's House was responsible for initiating spending bills, the Senate could refuse to support the spending. They represented the state governments, who would have to pony up the money if necessary.

Since the senators were elected by the state governments

they were very concerned that if they voted for spending that went over budget, their state treasuries would have to make up the difference, and this could lead to them not being reelected to their positions as senators.

As a result, getting spending bills through the senate was a tough rite of passage. It kept the size of the federal government in check.

When our system was put together, it was *sovereign states* which did so. They were all independent governments, but had agreed that they needed to stand together through the War for Independence and beyond. However, they all jealously guarded their sovereignty when forming the United States. The title of our country actually denotes this fact: the United *States*. Our name is actually calling out a *system*, as well as a country.

As far as we know, this was the first time this had been done. Since this time, other revolutionary countries have followed suit (Union of Soviet Socialist Republics, People's Republic of whatever, and others which were rarely republics in practice, only in name).

Setting up the Congress in the manner the Founders did was designed to keep the powers of the states intact and prevent the growth of the federal government into a draconian entity. The Founders had studied history, and knew the tendency of government to grow well beyond its original limits, until it becomes a power only unto itself.

As time went by, the people became more imbued with the idea of a national government rather than a federated one of the states.

For many years, even lasting into the early 20th century, when people were asked where they were from they often answered that they were a citizen of — then say the state. (I am a citizen of New York, Oregon, or Ohio.) As the loss of state sovereignty grew, this manner of speaking faded away.

By 1900, the people were educated to believe that changes needed to be made to move our system toward a democracy rather than a strict republic.

One of the changes that was made was the Sixteenth Amendment, which allowed an income tax. Keep in mind, again, that the *second plank* of *The Communist Manifesto* is the establishment of a progressive income tax. *The significance of this is that it was a primary step toward the establishment of a communist government.*

Prior to this change made in the Constitution, it was illegal for the federal government to tax the people directly. The Founders understood the tremendous control that this taxing power would have given to the government over every individual citizen and business.

They understood that such an income tax would give inordinate power to the government, and that there would be little barrier to the government taxing as they saw fit for whatever they saw fit, and giving it to whom or whatever they saw fit.

A direct tax on the people and businesses would bypass the states and allow the federal government to grow to a very large size. It would also give the federal government political control over people and businesses through a system of tax deductibility. Those who were friends of the government's policies received tax deductibility, and those who were not friends of the government's policies did not.

This became a serious problem during the Obama administration, when they withheld deductibility from conservative organizations such as the Tea Parties, groups investigating voter fraud, etc.

On the other hand, deductibility was extended to organizations which were allies of the administration, including groups that promoted gun control legislation.

Ultimately, the Marxists in America convinced enough people that an income tax was necessary in light of the growing desire to expand government "to help the people," and the Constitution was changed with Amendment Sixteen.

After this, the federal government no longer looked to the states to pay for overruns in the budget, and the entire process was reversed to where the federal government started to help finance the states. This then gave power over the states to the federal government. Thus, the check and balance between the states and the federal government, known as federalism, was broken.

At the same time two other changes were made which destroyed the legs on which the Republic stood: The establishment of the Federal Reserve and Amendment Seventeen.

The Federal Reserve fills plank number five of *The Communist Manifesto* for establishing a communist government. It centralized the banking and monetary system and gave power to unidentified bankers over the finances of the country, all in the name of controlling the bankers.*

In addition to the income tax, the manner in which the government started to tax the people was by using inflation created through the Federal Reserve. Inflation of the money supply over the course of a century has reduced the value of a dollar to one cent.

In other words, the federal government has robbed the people of 99% of the value of their money. What cost a dollar in 1914 now costs the people, basically, one hundred dollars.

It is an invisible tax. All the people know is that prices keep going up, and they blame the businessman rather than the government.

The socialist economist John Maynard Keynes, used by the Council on Foreign Relations to promote his policies of inflation, wrote:

> By a continuing process of inflation, governments can confiscate, secretly and unobserved, an important part of the wealth of their citizens …. There is no subtler, no surer means of overturning the existing basis of society than to debauch the currency. The process engages all the hidden forces of economic law on the side of destruction, and does it in a manner which not one man in a million is able to diagnose ….
>
> — *The Economic Consequences of the Peace,* 1919

* For the full story of the creation of the Federal Reserve and the conspiracy that created it, see *In the Shadows of the Deep State*, or for a more comprehensive look at the Fed, see *The Creature From Jekyll Island*, by G. Edward Griffin. Both are available from ShopJBS.org

Keynes always recommended to the federal government under Franklin Roosevelt to function with an economic system using inflation.

This system established, due to the ignorance of the American people, the Marxist plan of a direct attack on the property of each individual American, robbing them of the value of their property, if for no other reason than the value of their property hinged on the medium of exchange: the dollar.

Over the last century we have seen many businessmen and bankers cooperate with the communist movement toward a one-world government. Americans ask themselves, "Why?" The reason is that in the long run, it isn't business, property, or money that is the aim, it is power. You can have all of the money in the world, but in the end it will mean nothing if the power is in someone else's hands.

Mao Zedong said that power comes from the barrel of a gun, meaning that whoever has control of the army or an armed force will have the power. No amount of money will be able to go against that kind of power.

This is why our forefathers used the expression, "Keep your powder dry."

Further, if a group has control of all property, they have the power to negate any consortium of bankers or businessmen. Therefore, power in and of itself is the defining motivation of those who mean to rule. If they hold the power, they do not need money. Here's a clue: Hitler was poor. Stalin was poor. Mao was poor. Once they held the power, they didn't need to hold the money power, although they found it useful from time to time.

Communism isn't about spreading the wealth — it is about the accumulation of power. This is the key to why certain businessmen, who should be against communism, actually support it. Many of these businessmen or their companies belong to organizations that want a New World Order.

Never think that the "money power" is the real source of our problems. It is a useful tool, but not the endgame.

# Chapter Nine

# THE RIGHT OF THE PEOPLE TO BE SECURE

The Fourth Amendment of the Bill of Rights states:

> The right of the people to be secure in their persons, houses, papers, and effects, against unreasonable searches and seizures, shall not be violated, and no warrants shall issue but upon probable cause, supported by oath or affirmation, and particularly describing the place to be searched, and the persons or things to be seized.

Here we see a direct admonition by our Founders to protect property and the need to have a firm legal process in play in order for a government authority to even enter a home.

We used to say that a man's home is his castle. This meant that no one, especially the government, could invade his home arbitrarily. The Fourth Amendment affirms that right.

Yet we see that this is not always the case these days with the laws that have been passed and the arbitrary manner in which some federal law enforcement agencies operate. The recent pandemic and the edicts issued by governors and others have actually eroded the Fourth Amendment's protections.

Again, fear has been used to convince people they can ignore the Constitution.

How? Let us look at the reverse of the idea that government cannot come into your home without just cause.

In many states the people were told to quarantine themselves in their homes for a specific amount of time. What if they didn't? How would it have been enforced?

Many sheriffs and chiefs of police refused to enforce such edicts, declaring that they didn't have the manpower or that the edicts were unconstitutional. However, some were forced by their mayors or governors to enforce the decrees against businesses who stated they would remain open and not quarantine.

Churches were not allowed to meet. In some cities, such as New York and Los Angeles, they were threatened to be shut down permanently if they met in violation of the edict. In some places churchgoers were not even allowed to park in their church parking lot with their windows shut and participate in the services by radio.

Yet the First Amendment states that "Congress shall make no law respecting an establishment of religion, or prohibiting the free exercise thereof…." It is the first thing mentioned — the most important thing to our Founders. Yet for the first time in our history, the celebration of Easter was forbidden.

This is a stark example of the erosion of the Bill of Rights.

Our Founders dealt with diseases that flowed through the population, but never dreamt of isolating the healthy people. They, as everyone down through the centuries had done, quarantined the sick. Our Founders had to deal with smallpox, yellow fever, cholera, etc. These were not unusual occurrences, yet our forefathers did not isolate the healthy from each other or curtail their freedom.

Quarantine is when you restrict the movement of sick people.

Tyranny is when you restrict the movement of healthy people.

Examples abound of the ridiculous edicts and their limitations: No church, but marijuana outlets, liquor stores, grocery stores, and abortion clinics could all stay open. It was not unusual for local politicians to disobey their own edicts and justify their actions based on their own importance. These same politicians had no problem having the police protect their own property but not the property being burned to the ground by arsonists during "peaceful" demonstrations.

The demonstrators never practiced "social distancing," some wearing face masks and some not.

Local authorities in some cities had no problem with leftist demonstrators violating their edicts regarding wearing masks or "social distancing"; it was just the religious, ordinary people that had to obey.

At any rate, what we are demonstrating is the deterioration of the Bill of Rights relative to the movement and assembly of people and their property rights.

The first five steps in the *Manifesto* toward communizing a country deal directly with property. All of them do so directly or indirectly, such as intellectual property, one's labor, etc. Labor is also a form of property — a man's time and effort are his own property, unless he is a slave.

Our government has implemented step four in the *Manifesto*, the confiscation of property of those accused of certain crimes, using the RICO Act and other federal laws. Often, those found innocent never are able to fully recover the property confiscated from them, because it has been sold, lost, or destroyed. While the idea is to punish criminals and not allow them to enjoy the fruits of their crimes, too many innocent people have found themselves embroiled in lawsuits trying to recover their property, to no avail.

As an example, in 2020 there was a case in Arizona in which a girl borrowed her boyfriend's Jeep while he was at work, and without his knowledge used it to go and sell $25 worth of marijuana. She was caught and arrested, and the Jeep confiscated. The boyfriend was entirely innocent of the crime and the charges were dropped against her, yet the government wanted him to pay $1,900 to get his Jeep back. It was all done under the Arizona Civil Asset Forfeiture law.

This is a problem when it comes to gun confiscations in violation of the Second Amendment. It is a real problem for private citizens to recover confiscated guns from government agencies in many parts of the country. The reasons for the confiscation vary, sometimes making sense, and at other times being arbitrary acts by police agencies at the behest of leftist attorneys general, many elected with the financial help of the likes of billionaire leftist manipulator George Soros.

In the West, there are cases where people have used their guns to defend themselves and found themselves in a great deal of trouble. Some of these cases involve the draconian edicts of government over the use of land and the attempts to confiscate the land in the name of the environment or land-use regulations.

People have defended their homes from violent mobs and had their guns confiscated, and then been charged for daring to defend their property. We return to the couple in St. Louis, Mark and Patricia McCloskey, who did just this. The Circuit Attorney of St. Louis ordered the police to confiscate the couple's guns. Then they were charged by the Circuit Attorney with exhibiting a semiautomatic rifle in "an angry or threatening manner," a felony that could have led to four years in prison. Finally the Missouri attorney general and the governor said they would intervene in favor of the McCloskeys, but as of this writing there is no word that they have. And, it is not clear whether the guns will be returned to the couple.

If they are returned to the McCloskeys it will be a plus, since when the authorities confiscated Mrs. McCloskey's pistol they found that it was inoperable, and repaired it. Apparently this was done to show the court that she was brandishing an operative pistol, when in fact it wasn't working at the time.

The McCloskeys had never left their premises in the course of defending their property and lives.

This example is no longer an isolated incident due to

the public riots and disorder displayed in 2020. Many local authorities did more to curtail citizens protecting their property then they did the rioters. This slowly changed as the public became more and more furious at their local governments. Politicians do want to be reelected.

Property rights are extremely important to freedom. And, a person has the right to defend his property, even though such rights are steadily under attack by authoritarian government at all levels.

How does one defend his property? By any means possible, which usually means using a gun to do so.

Part of the reason for this book is to inform Americans what private property rights are and the need to defend them. The right of private property and the ownership of guns go hand in hand. They cannot be separated.

Not all property is tangible, and we start to explore this aspect of private property in the next chapter.

# Chapter Ten

# INTO A TRAP, AN EAR OF CORN AT A TIME

There is a story of how a local farmer enticed wild pigs into a trap.

The farmer put posts into the ground and in the middle of the posts he strewed ears of corn. The wild pigs came and saw no danger and ate the corn.

The next day, the farmer placed railings around a small amount of the posts and again sprinkled the ears of corn in the center. Since the area was still very open, the pigs had no fear and ate the corn.

Gradually the farmer added railings to all of the posts, and kept giving the pigs corn.

Finally, he attached a gate at the remaining opening of the railed posts and again placed corn in the center. Once the pigs went into the enclosure, he ran up and slammed the gate shut, capturing the pigs, which he smoked forthwith.

This is an analogy for how people can be suckered into accepting a free lunch without noticing that a price is always attached and without knowing what the ultimate price will be. There is no such thing as a free lunch.

However, there is always a price to pay for government largess, though it may look innocent. People have a weakness in not being able to predict what will happen in the future if they keep going down the same path.

What we see happening in America is the entrapment of the people. They do not understand that communist schemes will trap them as surely as the pigs in the preceding tale. The corn may be tasty, and they may not see the posts being driven into the ground around them, but at some point, the people will have to pay the price for having been trapped into something they cannot reverse.

Let us give an example of the wiles of those who mean to rule us in the long run. We will use an example from early in American history that will surprise you, since you were never taught it in school.

By their use of beguiling verbiage, Marxists have the ability to sell socialism and the strings that bind people down in a manner that not everyone can see through. As an example:

> We believe that government, like every other intelligent agency, is bound to do good to the extent of its ability — that it ought actively to promote and increase the general well-being — that it should encourage and foster Industry, Invention, Intellectual, Social and Physical Progress…. Such is our idea of the sphere of government.
>
> — Horace Greeley, 1850, *Horace Greeley and Other Pioneers of American Socialism*, by socialist historian Charles Sotheran, published in 1892

Recall that Horace Greeley was the publisher of the *New-York Tribune* newspaper and that he hired Marx for eleven years before and into the Civil War. Greeley was a leader in starting over 50 communist communes around America before the war, and when they waned as a movement they all registered with the Communist International.

For government to be involved as Greeley suggests, or those who profess not to be socialists but agree with those who are, means that government — not individual citizens — will decide what all of the improvements will be. It means that government will decide what are the "correct" industries and sciences, what inventions will go forward and be utilized, and the correct social and physical progress.

In the beginning, it can seem as if it is good for the government to be involved. But in order to accomplish these things, the government must build a bureaucracy to do them and then begin to regulate them. And, invention is actually stifled under government, since invention requires the freedom to think outside of the box. It is freedom *from* bureaucracy that leads to invention; that is why America has been more inventive than any other country, because it has been more free.

Indeed, many of the "American" inventions came about because those who immigrated here were able to think and invent and keep the fruits of their labor and intellect. They could not do so in the countries whence they came. They came to a *free* country and all that this word meant, and as a result they flourished.

At the minimum such designs as outlined by Greeley are fascist socialism, a welding of government and business, sometimes called *corporatism* today.

The process involves government planning. This may seem to be to the advantage of the citizens, but in the long run planning leads to full-scale socialism since the planning is done by the government. The government plans — the citizen obeys. It is the ultimate end of the road. This is inevitable and inescapable. The onset of planning by government is so deceptively benign that the average citizen cannot imagine where the process will lead and its ultimate end.

At first, planning will include citizens — citizens who generally agree with what the government bureaucracy wants. Such individuals will be put forward and promoted within the community. However, once people start to disagree with the real planners within the government, these citizens will be put to the side and other people promoted who "will stand for the community."

Most planning commissions even today are actually show business. By the time of the public hearings the plans have been laid and the show is started to move the citizens into compliance. If public reaction is too negative, they hold hearing after hearing until the people get tired of attending and then the government implements what they wanted all along since the opposition has, for all practical purposes, disappeared.

While the process was subtle, the idea that government could control thought and invention was beginning to take hold already during Greeley's life. People were already losing their appreciation and understanding of private property rights, not only in land but intellectual property.

Generally, the problem was not so much direct government involvement in the intellectual progress of the country, as it was the concerted efforts by Marxists to control it by subterfuge. This was accomplished by the infiltration of intellectual organizations such as historical societies, publishing companies, newspapers, colleges, etc.*

Over time, this government involvement replaced private control of intellectual property rights. As a result of the stifling of independent thought and publishing over a prolonged length of time, the people did not notice there was anything to be upset about.

The best portrayal of government taking away the right to even think, let alone produce something as a result of thinking, is the international best-seller *1984*, by George Orwell. The stifling of thought was accomplished by a number of means by which "Big Brother was watching," and you were not even allowed to think differently from the state let alone do anything with those thoughts. Even the property right to your own thoughts was eliminated. This is happening for real today.

Orwell worked with the communists before World War II and knew of their plans and where they were going and so wrote a number of fictional books to warn the reader of the

---

* One of the best sources for this aspect of history is the book *To the Victor Go the Myths & Monuments*, available at ShopJBS.org.

dangers of the communist world.

The process has begun in the United States with the controls and censorship of the Internet and mass media. Some may not be aware of how bad this censorship is because they do not post certain items online which can be taken down within hours, sometimes minutes — some videos get tens of thousands of views within hours and then, poof!, disappear from YouTube, Facebook, and Twitter.

It is not only the search engines that censor free speech. The Chinese, for instance, have somewhere between 50,000 and 100,000 hackers that work for the People's Liberation Army. Not only are they involved in stealing secrets from the militaries of various countries, but they steal industrial secrets as well. They are also involved in shutting down websites or information they deem adverse to the Communist Party line around the world.

For this reason the Trump administration outlawed the use of Chinese equipment, such as Huawei, in the United States. Many other countries have followed suit.

Freedom of speech includes the idea that this is an individual's intellectual property. This also is coming under increasing attack.

Part of the process of entrapping people is denying them the necessary information to understand the problem and offer solutions to the problem that are diverse and not "politically correct." In a free society, all sides should be brought forward, allowing decisions to be made by one or all.

In the case of gun legislation, one side receives more attention than the other due to censorship and/or distortion of the pro-Second Amendment side. Second Amendment supporters usually have to rely on independent organizations to disseminate their side of the story, as the media won't do it.

Social media also ban people who are pro-gun, saying that they are too radical if they pose with their gun. This occurs with Facebook all of the time.

Politicians understand the people are frustrated with the problems of private property rights, excessive taxation, etc. Although they use such frustration to enlist voter support for their candidacy or political party, however, they rarely remedy the problems.

Even if the people understand the problem, that doesn't mean they understand the remedy and are able to force politicians to heal our land, which we will take up next.

# Chapter Eleven

# POLITICS AS USUAL

Americans have become so used to free elections and looking to their elected officials to handle problems that they have ignored several very serious problems for some time.

Perhaps it is unfair to express it quite this way. A better way of expressing it is that they have been deliberately kept ignorant of problems that exist in our elective process, and have been inundated with schemes to solve *problems they do notice* that will only make the problems worse.

How can citizens decide on whom to support at the polls and how to make changes through their elected representatives?

The first place they can look is at the party platforms the political parties issue each election cycle. When it comes to the Second Amendment, the Republicans almost always declare their support for it. Increasingly, the Democrats tend to eliminate discussion of it entirely, since in some areas it is a very sore point to want to alter the right to keep and bear arms.

In any case, politicians have been chipping away at the Second Amendment for some time. What the politicians say and what they really mean are not always the same — for either major party. The steady erosion of the right to keep and bear arms in spite of the politicians' public support for the Second Amendment reveals the hypocrisy of what they say.

Party platforms are the show business of political parties; rarely are they followed. They occupy a great deal of time for party delegates at all levels of the party, but usually the "fix" is in by the leaders of the parties, even though they go through the motions of deciding on the platform. Having served on several party platforms, we can attest that this is the case, particularly the higher you go in the process, from county to state to national. Never forget that platform committee chairmen are appointed by the party leadership, not the delegates that form the platform committee. The chairmen then control a great deal of the process, if not all of it.

While this chapter heading is "Politics as Usual," perhaps we should say "Effective Politics." Effective politics takes work, but work that is effective and work that is organized.

The result of any election is based on the general knowledge level of the electorate. The voters will vote on the basis of their understanding of the American system and the issues at hand, as well as whether they can trust the candidates to perform as promised after elected.

The only way they can be assured of this, is to closely monitor the politicians' votes and positions on the issues.

We have seen countless people profess that they absolutely support the Second Amendment, and then later vote for things that infringe on that right. It takes not only an *informed* electorate, but an *organized* electorate to ensure that their representatives adhere to the Constitution in all things, not just the Second Amendment.

Generally speaking, a politician who abrogates the other

rights in the Bill of Rights will also do so with the Second Amendment, sooner or later.

We have shown how attacks on any one of the rights in the Bill of Rights can come back and influence the abrogation of the Second Amendment. Therefore, all of our rights have to be adhered to, or none will be adhered to in the long run.

One may doubt this assessment; however, can one deny that the loss of all of our rights would mean that we would also lose the right to keep and bear arms? At what point would we lose the Second Amendment with the loss of our other rights? Would it happen if we lost a third of them? What about half? Surely with the loss of 75 percent.

We have already lost a great deal of the rights which are spelled out in the Bill of Rights, either completely or partially. Let us give just one example of how much we have lost the First Amendment.

The First Amendment states:

> Congress shall make no law respecting an establishment of religion, or prohibiting the free exercise thereof; or abridging the freedom of speech or of the press; or the right of the people peaceably to assemble, and to petition the Government for a redress of grievances.

When the Bill of Rights was penned and ratified, there were only two methods of mass communication: speaking and printing. These were the methods used to communicate to the people, particularly in the political world.

Since that time, every means of communication invented has come under the regulation and control of the federal government: telegraph, telephone, radio, television, etc. This violates the spirit of the First Amendment.

Worse, the people never objected to these controls or thought of how they violated the spirit of the First Amendment.

Now we see that monopolies that control the Internet are engaging in wholesale censorship against those who disagree with government policy and/or are constitutionalists. They really clamp down on people who profess to believe in conspiracies, real or imagined.

The point is, we have lost a great deal of our freedom of "speech."

Relative to the freedom of religion and the ability to exercise that freedom, the pandemic of 2020 showed that the state governments could curtail this right. They enforced edicts as if they were law. The edicts were not "law," they were simply orders imposed by governors without the legislative process or even the input of the citizens.

This, for all practical purposes, was a war on Christianity and Judaism. It happened at the same time that Marxist demonstrators attacked churches, desecrating them and, in some cases, burning them down.

Those paying attention to the rabble in the streets during the pandemic of 2020 know it was not that unusual for the mob to chant against Christ or to chant other anti-religious slogans.

For the first time in our history, thanks to state or local

governments, Americans were not allowed to celebrate Easter, and were threatened with fines, jail, and/or permanent closure of the church if they met.

The sad part of this is that the vast majority of pastors and rabbis did not stand up and tell the government where they could take their edicts.

At the onset of the American Revolution, it was the pastors who helped lead the way. Today, they have been either heavily infiltrated by Marxism or they "don't want to get involved in politics."

Ask the pastor who stands by and watches while his church is being burned to the ground if he thinks that maybe he should have been involved. He already is, he just doesn't realize it. If you are the target, just because you don't realize it doesn't mean that you are not involved.

We can say the same regarding the rest of the First Amendment: the people were not allowed to peaceably assemble and petition the government for a redress of grievances. Why? Because when people can't get together to organize (assemble) they cannot bring people together to stop what the government is doing wrong.

The Internet will not work to do this. This medium may be able to get people out into the street, but it cannot be used to organize people to get things done effectively. If it could, all of our problems would have already been solved.

Note, however, that while we could not get together in churches and synagogues, the Marxists were allowed to mass in the streets, which led to violence. At first these violent events were not curtailed by most local authorities, and this led to many people losing their businesses and livelihood.

This demonstrated the lack of protection of property rights by local authorities. The reason for this was not that they were incompetent, but that those in charge were just as Marxist as the criminal crowds, having fooled the voters into electing them.

Commentator after commentator referred to the crowds as anarchists. Soon they realized that they were Marxists. Most called the local authorities incompetent. They never realized that perhaps the leaders of the street gangs were actually working with the local authorities behind the scenes, at least having the same goals if not being directed by the same Marxist leaders. One blatant example was New York. The mayor was a communist just as were the leaders in the streets.

In Seattle, where the Marxists took over several blocks in one neighborhood and terrorized the residences and businesses for several weeks, the mayor called it a Summer of Love.

In city after city, mayors forced their police departments to pull back and allow the mayhem to go forward. In addition, at least at first, many of the police were not even allowed to use equipment to protect themselves.

In all of these cities the Republicans blamed it on the fact that they were led by Democrats. They never mentioned that perhaps they were not Democrats, but Marxists. This was clear since their other policies in running the cities were Marxist.

These mayors were not incompetent, they were allowing the Marxist program of rebellion to go forward for their own political ends in a major election year.

Nowhere in the mass media, liberal or conservative, was the idea of foreign intervention brought up, even though the heads of the Department of Justice and FBI both stated that foreign powers were involved in the street violence.

It does not take much for the average person to go online and look up some of the organizations involved to see that they adhere to Maoism, meaning China was involved.*

We could spend a great deal of print to go down the rest of the Bill of Rights, but let us give only one more example that most will recognize immediately: the right to a speedy trial.

The Sixth Amendment says that "The accused shall enjoy the right to a speedy … trial…." This today is rare. For example, criminal trials are drawn out for years after the defendants are arrested. This author was a witness in a murder trial that took three years to commence. It was an open-and-shut case, with several witnesses who saw the murder take place in the middle of an apartment complex.

As a result of the 2020 mayhem, private citizens around the country started to protect their cities from destruction. In town after town, locals would be armed to stop the demonstrators. It was very rare that the media ever mentioned these events. They reported on singular events of a lone

---

* To see the extent of Chinese infiltration into the United States, we recommend the book *China: The Deep State's Trojan Horse in America,* which documents the influence of the Chinese Communist Party in a wide swath of American society, including communist street organizations. Available from ShopJBS.org.

gunman, but not when many in the neighborhood rose up to defend their property.

The incidents they did mention were isolated people who brandished weapons, such as in St. Louis, or actually fired upon demonstrators, such as in Kenosha, Wisconsin. These individuals were chastised in the media and by the government as if they were the criminals — as if they should have allowed their property and their own bodies to be destroyed.

In all of this was a blatant disregard for property rights and the right of self-defense.

Our Founders would weep.

The point is, there are many ways to negate the Second Amendment when it comes to the individual.

We need to also point out how the Second Amendment was drastically changed at the end of the Civil War.

At that time the state-controlled militias were replaced with the National Guard. The Guard still has some of the trappings of the original militia, but for all practical purposes is an arm of the national government—with a few state prerogatives. The name, *National* Guard, should say it all.

Some would dispute this analysis; however, National Guard personnel are paid by the federal government, not the states. They follow national standards. Their ranks of officers are appointed by Congress, not the state legislatures. And so forth.

One can argue that in today's world this is necessary. Nonetheless, the state militias no longer exist except as paper organizations from state to state, to be used during a time of emergency if their wing of the National Guard is deployed out of the state or country and is thus unavailable.

The point of all of this is that the Bill of Rights has been severely curtailed. At what point will this mean the total curtailment of the right of the individual to be armed?

Which leads us to the idea that perhaps those who are sincerely committed to the right to keep and bear arms should get involved in the program to protect *all* rights, not just the Second Amendment.

The Second Amendment will not protect you if you have lost all of your other rights.

It will certainly not protect you if you act alone. The saying on that bumper sticker that they will not get your gun until they pry it from your cold, dead hands will become a reality.

Why did our Founders put the Second Amendment into the Bill of Rights? They did so because they had just used their arms to secure their freedom from their own oppressive government, the British, and they wanted to make sure that they could do so again if the need arose.

An armed citizenry can determine whether the government remains limited and not oppressive. But, *this can only be done if the citizenry is organized to do so*, and organized in such a way that the use of arms will not ever become necessary.

Ask yourself if you have any clue how to organize your town to form a militia to stand up to oppression. The answer for most people is no. So that means that something needs to be done so that you will never have to stand up in this manner.

Finally, we promised early on an example of why we always have to be on guard to make sure those in whom we place our trust stay true to the causes they claim to support.

First, a little history. Forgive the length, but it is necessary to understand the background for what we will reveal and the seriousness of it. In 1970, Zbigniew Brzezinski wrote *Between Two Ages: America's Role in the Technetronic Era.* In it, he said:

> That is why Marxism represents a further vital and creative stage in the maturing of man's universal vision. Marxism is simultaneously a victory of the external, active man over the inner, passive man and a victory of reason over belief: it stresses man's capacity to shape his material destiny — finite and defined as man's only reality — and it postulates the absolute capacity of man to truly understand his reality as a point of departure for his active endeavors to shape it.

The entire book by Brzezinski was laudatory toward Marxism and how the communists "deviated" from it. This is a problem when you realize that all of socialism looks to Marx and the conspiratorial aspect of the elevation of Marx within the socialist/communist movement. Brzezinski also stated in his book that the United States was passé.

As a result of this book, David Rockefeller helped Brzezinski start the Trilateral Commission (TC), whose goal is to unite three areas — North America, Western Europe, and Japan — into a single entity as a step toward their New World Order.

Both men were members of the Council on Foreign Relations. Couple this with Rockefeller's admission in his autobiography that he was working for a world government, and you get the idea of the aims of the TC. In addition, Rockefeller was the chairman of the CFR for 15 years, and remained the honorary chairman until the day he died.

President James Carter, a member of the TC before he was elected president, named Brzezinski his head of National Security. It was Brzezinski who opened up the spigot of trade with China and facilitated the ties between American banks and Chinese banking.

Finally, we get to the point. At one time, the speaker of the House was Congressman Tom Foley from Spokane, Washington. He was a very "liberal" representative. He was also a homosexual, although he denied it. After he was defeated for reelection due to a few years of heavy education of the voters in his district about how he actually voted in Congress, he became the head of the Trilateral Commission. Everything he stood for was aimed at negating the independence of the United States.

Every election, the National Rifle Association sent bumper stickers out to their members in the mail for them to place on their cars in support of Foley.

It is not politics as usual, but *effective politics* that is needed to preserve our rights and freedoms, as we shall see in our conclusion.

# Chapter Twelve

# CONCLUSION

As we have shown, standing alone will not work. Yet each of us must do something if we are to save our Republic.

We have shown that all of our rights in the Bill of Rights are important, and that they are being abrogated a step at a time. What's important is not simply the preservation of the Second Amendment, but the preservation of the entire Bill of Rights.

How does one do this?

It cannot be done by working alone, you have to become involved with others to effect change.

We mentioned the example of Tom Foley, who was speaker of the House when he went down to defeat as a result of an organized, concerted campaign of educating the citizens about how he voted in Congress. The actual aim of the initiative was not to get him out of office, it was to influence him to vote differently, to honor the Constitution. Once he would not do that, enough of the voters rejected him.

It is all determined by how the people vote. It has become obvious that too many people vote who do not understand the basic principles of Americanism and the Constitution. If they did, they would elect people who also understood the Constitution.

First, do not think in terms of political party — which

one is better than the other. They are all bad and our Founders knew this, especially George Washington. In his Farewell Address, once taught to every school boy in the country, he warned about being caught up in factions, what we would call political parties today.

He had great insight and knew that over time they would tear the country apart in their quest for power. It is human nature.

James Madison addressed the problem as well:

> The accumulation of all powers, legislative, executive, and judiciary, in the same hands, whether of one, a few, or many, and whether hereditary, self-appointed, or elective, may justly be pronounced the very definition of tyranny.
>
> — *The Federalist Papers*, #47

It does not matter whether the faction is a political party or an organization such as the Council on Foreign Relations, which has members in both parties and has permeated government, academia, media, etc., the principle applies.

The solution is in the understanding of the electorate. When the majority of voters understand history and the principles on which our country was founded, and have within them the love of not only country but of these principles, then the representation from these voters' areas will be sound.

Today, due to a number of factors, not the least of which is a poor educational system pertaining to Americanist principles, the voters on too many occasions send some of the worst people to Congress and their state legislatures.

There is only one solution for this, and that is to change the voters' understanding. This may seem a huge task, but it is one that can be accomplished provided people who already understand band together to get the job done. And, it doesn't have to be in every congressional district, just enough of them to constitute a majority in Congress.

Once the people in Congress start to see which way the wind is blowing, the opportunists will swing over because, after all, they want to be reelected.

The same applies to the media and every other aspect of American society. Once the people start to understand, they will reject media outlets, colleges, etc., that spew the Marxist line and that will go bankrupt if they do not change. Institutions that promote Americanism will flourish.

In educating people on our Americanist principles, one person educating others becomes two, two become four, four become eight, and so on. Can you imagine what 500 could do in a congressional district?

The education must be concerted and have the tools necessary to get the job done. Pamphlets, booklets, books, videos, speakers, and all the various means to educate others must be produced and disseminated.

But education without action leads to frustration.

Once people are educated, they must be organized into action campaigns to further the knowledge of people and to work against, or for, a variety of issues to help change government and further spread understanding.

And, as one wag expressed it, you don't want to be the best-informed person in a concentration camp saying, "I told you so."

So, the voters need to be educated. Who will do that, if you do not?

You may have a desire to do something, but you know that you cannot do it alone. Where does one go to get involved in the process and find others who want the same thing that you do?

Let us begin by pointing out that the mass media and leftist politicians often make out those who support the Second Amendment as Neanderthals. And that is when they are being polite! Second Amendment supporters have been called every name under the sun.

They do this to all who stand up for good government and the Constitution, including The John Birch Society. They have called the JBS everything —including racist, Nazi, KKK, even communist — everything they could think of to get people to reject the JBS and prevent them from looking closer at what it stands for.

The reason for this is that very early on, the communists realized that they had a new boy on the block that they had never experienced before. An organization designed to educate and activate the American people into a force like no other. One that would tell the truth no matter what and forge ahead against those who would tear down our Republic.

And, name names — expose the organizations and individuals who are out to change our country into a Marxist cog in the wheel of the New World Order.

The basic mission of The John Birch Society is to protect the Constitution and independence of the American people. Few can object to that. Where the JBS gets into trouble is when we identify those who are opposed to this agenda.

We take oaths to protect the Constitution from all enemies, foreign and domestic, when we sign up for our armed forces or serve in public office. The trouble is that we are told who the foreign enemies are, but not who the domestic enemies are. The John Birch Society tells who they are — and the domestic enemies don't like it.

That is the basic reason for the attacks against the JBS over the years and why they have tried to silence us for decades, and continue to censor us on the Internet today.

Yet we go about our business, informing and educating people on the basic principles of our country. The program is so successful that when we achieve a membership of approximately 500 in a congressional district, things start to change, from local government up to Congress.

The educational efforts of our members across a wide spectrum of society, from friends and family to local opinion molders, create a synergy that is difficult to stop. Our ad hoc committees in support of our local police and other initiatives bear fruit, too.

The efforts of each individual member vary. Some members are super active, others do what they can when they can, but with all working in concert on the same things at the same time, there is quite a rippling effect within the community.

One of the things we are busy doing is showing the difference between a republic and a democracy, with the idea of keeping our Republic intact. The understanding of the difference between the two and the fact that we are a republic was almost lost before the JBS started to educate people far and wide about this.

We believe that we have set back the communist program and timetable a minimum of 50 years due to our efforts. The communists' aim is to rule the world, and they cannot do so without subjugating America. The American people can stop the communists if they are aware of the problems, heal their own land, and prevent the New World Order being imposed on every living human being. It does not take a war. It takes disseminating knowledge.

Isn't it better to throw a book at someone rather than a bullet?

People will do the right thing once they understand what is going on and have the basis for building back the Republic with the correct solutions. We have to go around the media in order to do this.

We know that every member of the Society on average influences 100 voters. Some cannot even influence their spouse, others influence hundreds, sometimes thousands if they are in a position to do so. It all averages out to a ratio of 1:100.

With such a force, people will once again appreciate the need to support the Second Amendment and the rest of the

Bill of Rights.

One of the nice things about working with like-minded people is the camaraderie that is involved — being with friends who agree with you and work with you.

The burden is lifted of having to try to do it all alone. There are people just waiting for you to get on board to work together with.

And, if you don't do it, who will?

This is a battle to save our wonderful country for our children and grandchildren.

Come visit us at JBS.org.

# INDEX

# ABOUT THE AUTHOR

**Arthur R. Thompson** was born in Seattle, Washington, in 1938. He attended the University of Washington, the Washington Military Academy, and several art and design schools, and served as an officer in the Select Reserve Force of the Army National Guard. He worked for Boeing for several years, then published an intelligence newsletter after he worked in tandem with the Police Intelligence Squad in his metropolitan area, where he helped stop planned riots in the inner city by communist groups. He helped the police infiltrate area communist organizations, and learned their strategies and tactics.

From 1982 to 1995, Thompson created and led small manufacturing businesses, which took him all over the United States and Western Europe. He also went to Europe on a political fact-finding tour for The John Birch Society in 1989, at which time he witnessed the Berlin Wall coming down and became acquainted with many businessmen, academics, and members of the West German Cabinet and the European Community (which became the European Union).

Mr. Thompson served on his small town's city council and as chairman of his local Chamber of Commerce, worked as an official and elector for the Republican Party, and was a local leader in the State of Washington for the Christian Coalition.

Before and after his years in manufacturing, he served on the staff of The John Birch Society, and was CEO for 15 years, until 2020. While his children live in the Pacific Northwest, Mr. Thompson resides in Appleton, Wisconsin, with his wife, Joanne.

**Other books Mr. Thompson has written include:**

- *The UN's Agenda 2030: Marxist Stealth Plan For World Government*
- *China: The Deep State's Trojan Horse in America*
- *The United Nations: Unity Through Tyranny*
- *In the Shadows of the Deep State: A Century of Council on Foreign Relations Scheming for World Government*
- *To the Victor Go the Myths & Monuments: The History of the First 100 Years of the War Against God and the Constitution, 1776-1876, and Its Modern Impact*
- *International Merger by Foreign Entanglements*

The Official Store of The John Birch Society

To order extra copies of this book, go to
ShopJBS.org or call 1-800-342-6491

# How Can I Make a Difference?

**GETTING STARTED IS AS EASY AS 1,2,3**

**1**
**Sign up for JBS news and action alerts**
• Stay informed with free content
• Visit www.JBS.org/e-newsletter to sign up now

**2**
**Contact your elected representatives**
• Local, state, and federal officials represent you
• Visit www.JBS.org/act-now for contact information

**3**
**Join The John Birch Society**
• National concerted action multiplies your impact
• Visit www.JBS.org/join to apply for membership today

# The John Birch Society

P.O. Box 8040
Appleton, WI 54912-8040
(920) 749-3780 • **JBS**.org

"Less government, more responsibility,
and — with God's help — a better world."